6th edition

crossover

1

von
Peadar Curran

in Zusammenarbeit
mit der Verlagsredaktion

Ausgabe Baden-Württemberg
für berufliche Gymnasien

Workbook

KLASSE 11

Cornelsen

Topic 1

Words in context	4
Getting to grips with grammar	7
Stats & pics: A question of faith	10
Song	11
Literature	12
Going deeper	14
Fun & games	15

Topic 2

Words in context	17
Getting to grips with grammar	20
Song	22
Writing workshop	23
Stats & pics: Talking about cartoons	25
Going deeper	26
Fun & games	27

Topic 3

Words in context	29
Getting to grips with grammar	32
A political speech	34
Stats & pics: The general election 2019	35
Writing workshop: Writing a comment	36
Going deeper	38
Fun & games	39

Topic 4

Words in context	41
Getting to grips with grammar	44
Stats & pics: Internet usage	46
Writing workshop: Writing a summary	47
Mediation: A question of trust	49
Going deeper	50
Fun & games	51

Skills

Writing a comment	53
Doing a creative writing task	55
Analysing and describing charts and graphs	57
Presenting	58
Dealing with listening tasks	59
Using dictionaries	61
Stylistic devices	62
Describing and analysing cartoons and pictures	64
Analysing a text	67

Appendix

Audio transcripts	70

🔊 Dieses Symbol weist auf Hörtexte hin, die Sie in der PagePlayer-App finden. Laden Sie die kostenlose App herunter, wählen Sie **Crossover 6th edition Ausgabe Baden-Württemberg Band 1** aus und scannen Sie die jeweilige Seite bzw. rufen Sie den Hörtext im Medienmenü auf.

Words in context

1 **a** Read the article on how people feel about being a teen today.

Is being a teenager harder today than in the past? We asked some teenagers and adults.

to **underestimate sth/sb** *unterschätzen*

AS-Levels/A-Levels *britische Entsprechung des Abiturs*

continuous assessment *kontinuierliche Beurteilung*

compared to *im Vergleich zu*

overwhelmed *überfordert*

to **treat sb/sth** *jdn/ etw behandeln*

consequence *Auswirkung*

climate change *Klimawandel*

issue *[hier] Problem*

mentally *psychisch*

imagine *sich vorstellen*

to **bully** *mobben*

to **suffer** *leiden*

violence *Gewalt*

comprehensive school *Gesamtschule*

anonymous *anonym*

impact *Auswirkung*

wellbeing *Wohlbefinden*

physical education (PE) *Sportunterricht*

challenge *Herausforderung*

to **get to grips with sth** *etw in den Griff bekommen*

on balance *alles in allem*

approach to sth *Herangehensweise an etw*

in terms of *im Sinne von*

opportunity *Gelegenheit*

empowered *ermächtigt*

I think people underestimate big time how stressful being a teenager is nowadays. I had my AS-levels last year, have to take my A-Levels next year, and, with continuous assessment, it feels like every week there's a deadline I have to meet. Compared to me, my parents had it easy. But when I try to relax on my phone, my parents nag me about 'screen time' and getting more fresh air. If I think about the world's problems too, and how a lot of people (including some of my friends) think we should all live up to Greta or Malala, I feel overwhelmed.

Tom D., 17, Liverpool, UK

I hate being called a 'teenager' – we are young adults and shouldn't be treated like children. I'm old enough to leave school, get married and mature enough to have a baby (if I wanted to). I don't think being a teenager is more or less difficult now than in the past. My parents were afraid of nuclear war when they were my age. Our generation have our own problems to face: the consequences of climate change and other global issues, and we have a part to play in making a positive future. We are young, but that doesn't mean we shouldn't make our voices heard.

Alice M, 16, Dublin, Ireland

As an older person and parent, I think most adolescents in Western countries have a physically easier life than, say, I had, but not mentally. Everything is much too intense! I couldn't imagine being a teen now – always online, always posting everything they do, never wanting to miss out on anything. Peer pressure and bullying doesn't stop when they get home any longer. Take my son, for example. He was bullied. He didn't suffer violence or verbal abuse at his comprehensive school, though – it was online: anonymous posts and threats on social media. It has had a huge impact on his self-esteem. In my opinion, teaching teenagers how to take care of their mental wellbeing should be made part of their compulsory physical education at secondary level.

Miriam A, 46, Portsmouth, UK

I think adolescence has always been a vulnerable time as young people face the anxiety and challenges of getting to grips with their identities and their role in the adult world. On balance though, I think our society's increased acceptance of diversity and tolerant approach to equality in terms of gender, sexual orientation and race means that this generation of young people will have much greater opportunities to actually be who they really are. Today's adolescents are more empowered and independent than before, authority figures such as teachers or parents have even less influence on them, but they have some powerful role models in their peers and I feel that's positive.

Dr Joyce S., 52, Melbourne, Australia

5

10

15

20

25

30

35

40

crossover 6th edition

ANSWER KEY

Words in context

1 b
1. Alice
2. Dr Joyce
3. Miriam
4. Tom

2 a
to take an exam: eine Prüfung ablegen
to nag sb: My mum always nags me to take my shoes off when I come home.
to live up to: einer Anforderung gerecht werden, etw. erfüllen
mature: reif
to have a baby: ein Kind bekommen
to face a problem
peer pressure: Gruppenzwang
verbal abuse: Beleidigung
threat: Drohung
self-esteem: If you have low self-esteem, then you do not feel good about yourself and your appearance.
compulsory: School uniforms are compulsory in many English-speaking countries.
vulnerable: verletzbar
anxiety
independent: WORD FAMILY: to depend on sth/sb, independence (noun)
authority figure: Autoritätsperson

2 b
1. face (problems)
2. nags
3. mature
4. vulnerable
5. threats
6. live up to
7. peer pressure
8. self-esteem

2 c
1. had
2. take
3. have
4. get
5. get
6. take

2 d
1. compulsory
2. verbal abuse
3. consequence
4. suffer
5. authority figures
6. anxiety

2 e
1. This is when other people think you have done something good.
2. When you have to do something by a certain time.
3. This means something difficult and good that you have done.
4. This is when you are able to do everything yourself and don't need your parents to help.
5. This is work that volunteers do to help people in their town or village.

Getting to grips with grammar

1
Luke: 's coming / 's putting
Kim: 'm looking forward
Oliver: need / Do you have
Luke: do you think
Oliver: sounds
Kim: don't like / prefer / know
Oliver: imagine / seems / are you looking
Luke: 'm doing / remember / forget
Kim: are you laughing / see
Luke: means / don't think / want
Luke: love

2
a. 'll be / 's going to rain
b. 're going to win / will win
c. 'll get / is going to fall
d. 's going to ask / won't say
e. 's going to turn off / 'll take

3 a
1. an/a
2. a/an
3. a/an
4. an/a
5. an/an
6. an/a

3 b
1. school / the school
2. hospital / the hospital
3. the prison / prison
4. college / the college

3 c
the city – fun – the Brauns – the people – the German – the accents – the books – school – the US – the one – the family – meat – family – the day – the mall – the weather – the countryside – nature – school – the school subjects – the latest

Stats & pics: A question of faith

1
It is a bar chart.

2
It shows the percentages of young people who believe in a god and who don't.

3

The number of religious young people decreased slightly. The number of spiritual young people also went down. The atheist/agnostic group is the biggest. This group grew between 2013 and 2020. The number of people who don't know or don't stay remained the same.

4

That young people are becoming less religious and spiritual.

Song

1

a line 5
b line 11
c lines 16/17
d line 28

2

a Be honest and people will listen (lines 13–14)
b Be nice to yourself (line 18)

3

I think the letter makes me feel worse. The father says the son should be honest and be who he really is, but it isn't easy to do that. It also says the son will have a hero's death – that doesn't sound so good.

4

Everyone on social media is so hyper and mean,
So give yourself a break, man, and turn off your screen!

Literature

1

a False
b False
c True
d True
e False
f False

2

1C, 2A, 3D, 4B

3

a … are not very clear and difficult to follow.
b Frances says in brackets that she was not prepared for the question about The Catcher in the Rye, even though she mentioned the book in her personal statement.
c she realises as she is speaking that studying English literature is really not what she wants to do in her heart.

4

I think it means that, at my age, my parents or teachers can give me tips for my future but it is very important that I myself really believe in what I choose to do.

5 a

Dear Ben,
I failed my interview for Cambridge University. But guess what? I'm not sad about it at all. Actually, I'm really happy! In the interview I realised that studying English literature isn't for me. I've decided to apply to art college instead because that is really what I've always loved. What about you? Email me soon!
Love, Frances

5 b

FRANCES   Hi Mum, I think I failed my interview.
MUM   Really? Why do you say that?
FRANCES   I wasn't able to answer the interviewers' questions. Even the simple questions. I didn't have a good reason to say why I wanted to study English literature.
MUM   But why not Frances? I thought you wanted to go to Cambridge.
FRANCES   Mum, I think I wanted to go there because you and everybody at school expected me to go there. But I know now that I want to study art and become an artist.
MUM   Frances, I believe in you and if that is what you want, I support you.
FRANCES   Thanks, Mum.

Going deeper

2

Mentioned: Applying to college, negative stereotypes of teens, climate change, youth unemployment, peer pressure

3

1c, 2a, 3b, 4c

4

a twice as high
b is increasing / growing / getting worse/bigger
c disagree / don't agree / argue; agree

Fun & games

1 a

Jay-Z – One – Said – Equality – Progressive – Hip-hop

2

no cap
open crib
(cringe) to feel embarrassed or ashamed about something
bae
(fresh) cool and fashionable, trendy
lit
ghost

(lost) this describes somebody who has no idea or only stupid ideas, somebody who is very uncool
throw shade
boots

3

										¹S	E	R	I	²O	U	³S
	⁴W	E	I	R	⁵D									U		E
⁶S					I									T		L
E				⁷E	A	S	Y	G	O	⁸I	N	G		F		
N		⁹F			H				N		O			I		
¹⁰S	T	U	B	B	O	R	N		T		I			S		
I		N			N				R		N			H		
B				E				O			G					
L		¹¹S	E	N	S	I	T	I	V	E						
E				T				E			¹⁵M					
	¹²S		¹³Q			¹⁴N	E	R	V	O	U	¹⁷S				
	M		U				T				O	I				
¹⁶P	A	S	S	I	O	N	A	T	E		D	L				
	R		E				D				Y	L				
	T		T									Y				

Topic 2

Words in context

1 b
1 True
2 False – There is a lot of development/gentrification and renovation.
3 True
4 False – All Dubliners agree that it is awful.
5 False – They are moving out so they can buy cheaper houses, but work in the city.

2 a
to grow up: aufwachsen
inner city: Innenstadt/innerstädtisch
close-knit community: My family and our neighbours are a close-knit community.
to be plagued by sth/sb
gentrification: Gentrifizierung
to catch up with sb/sth: jdn/etw einholen
suburb
amenity: Einrichtung
rural: There are many large farms in rural areas in Germany.
to commute: pendeln
property
accent: Akzent, Dialekt
public transport: Public transport in Germany is normally very reliable.
to serve: jdm/etw dienen
congestion: Verkehrsbelastung, Stau

2 b
unite/divide
detached/terraced
urban/rural
well-maintained/rundown

2 c
1e, 2d, 3a, 4f, 5c, 6b

2 d
1 industrial estate	5 village
2 suburb	6 countryside
3 public housing	7 capital
4 high-rise	8 borough

2 e
1 a national holiday	4 scenery
2 indigenous (people)	5 colonialism
3 picturesque	6 custom

Getting to grips with grammar

1

opened	built
have been	finished
closed down	hasn't shone
has been	has affected
have bought	was
have knocked down	moved in
have lived	have already missed
has made	

2

larger than / smaller than
the biggest / as big as
as sunny as / the sunniest
higher than / the most expensive

3 a
1 Did you know
2 Have you ever taken
3 Does Dublin have
4 Are they building
5 Have rental costs risen
6 Should Sydney introduce

3 b
| 1 isn't it | 3 didn't they |
| 2 has she | 4 do they |

3 c
1 When did Canberra become the capital of Australia?
2 How many people live in Dublin?
3 What are they building?
4 How much does a short-journey ticket cost on the London Underground?
5 Where / In which country is Wellington?
6 Who painted that graffiti?

Song

1

old buildings replaced by underground car parks
(ll.2–4).
buildings that have been demolished (ll.5–8).
bars and shops that have been turned into apartments
(ll.16–17)

2

I think he is talking about the city as it was when he
kissed somebody under the streetlight and also his
younger life.

3

I think the singer feels bad about the effects of the gold
rush. He has good memories of the person he kissed
but the old places where he was with the person are all
gone. The imagery is dark and negative: shadows,
haunts, ghosts, constructions sites and wreckage. He is
depressed that everything has changed.

Writing workshop

2

1 False – They are only going to build a playground for
   very young children.
2 False – The author got the project plans from the
   district council.
3 True
4 True
5 False – He wants every local teenager to email
   Declan Flynn, the head of planning in the council.

3

More formal	More informal
enquire	ask (about sth)
request	ask (for sth)
construct	build
obtain	get
provide	give
people	guys
relax	chill
mention	say sth about sth
require	need
demolish	trash
would like	want
will not	won't
consequently	so

4

1 as a result of
2 result in
3 leading to
4 Although
5 Nevertheless
6 Consequently
7 Due to

5

Dear Mr Flynn
I am writing to request that you protect our local skate
park.
Greenfield Ltd want to demolish the park and
construct apartments on it.
The park has provided teenagers with a place to meet
and relax for years.
Young people like me are not going to have anywhere
to spend our free time.
Greenfield obtained permission from you for their plans.
Consequently, we would like you to change that
permission so that Greenfield will have to keep the
skate park or construct a new one.

Stats & pics: Talking about cartoons

Describing a cartoon

1 black and white
2 background
3 depicts
4 look
5 in (the cartoon)
6 countryside
7 map
8 caption

Interpreting a cartoon

1 The cartoonist is making a sarcastic comment on the
   behaviour of city people who visit the countryside.
2 The cartoonist is ridiculing people who go to the
   countryside but cannot relax and enjoy it.
3 The point the cartoon is making seems to be that
   we are not able to take a break from our electronic
   devices.
4 The artist is criticizing the behaviour of those who
   worry about their phone signal instead of enjoying
   nature.

Giving your opinion

In my opinion, the cartoonist is successful/unsuccessful
in his/her portrayal of modern society because it
portrays the young couple as being stupid because
they are completely unprepared for a trip to the
countryside – this means anyone who is like those
people would not like the cartoon or its message.

Going deeper

1

congestion charges: S
fines and penalties: S
traffic calming: C
blocking motor traffic from streets: S
cheap public transport: C
park and ride schemes: C
cycle lanes: C
low-emission zones: S

2

1C, 2A

3

Protesters think: B, D
The city council thinks: A, E

4

1 can drive – longer
2 shorter than
3 longer
4 majority – reduce
5 do not own

Fun & games

1

odd-numbered	well-tended
council-built	semi-detached
high-rise	love-hate
close-knit	long-delayed

2 a

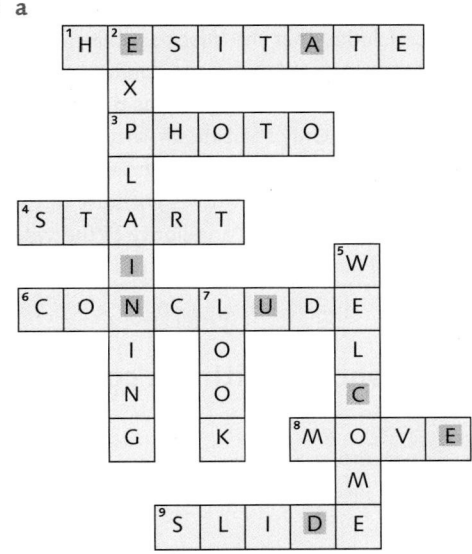

2 b

You've been a great audience!

3

1 home   4 door
2 kitchen   5 roof
3 house   6 wall

1f, 2c, 3b, 4d, 5a, 6e

4 a

1A, 2U, 3C, 4K, 5L, 6A, 7N, 8D

4 b

Auckland

Words in context

1 b

A Make voting compulsory.
B 10% of candidates should be aged between 18 and 30.
C More power to elected local government and more referenda
D Automatic voter registration on everyone's eighteenth birthday
E The best defence is a free press and a fair legal system.

2 a

turnout: Wahlbeteiligung
election: WORD FAMILY: to elect sb (as sth, to sth) (v), elected (adj), election (n)
polling station
to tally: (Stimmen) auszählen
eligible: berechtigt
to campaign
constituency: Wahlkreis
to represent sth/sb: WORD FAMILY: representative (n), representation (n), representative (adj)
to register
(an absentee) ballot: Stimmzettel
to stand for election: Angela Merkel stood for election for the last time in the 2017 German federal elections.
to overcome an obstacle
disenfranchisement: Wahlrechtsentzug
to exercise 'people power'
referendum: Referendum, Volksabstimmung

2 b

1 eligible/elections
2 ballots
3 represents/constituency
4 stand for election
5 register

2 c

1 polling station   5 disenfranchisement
2 MP   6 to tally
3 turnout   7 referendum
4 outcome

2 d

a Executive
b Legislative
c Judicial

Getting to grips with grammar

1

must be held
are not elected by
is decided by
has to be approved by
is passed by
must be signed by
can be removed by
is called
was impeached
was not supported by
was found

2

1 wasn't allowed to
2 'll be able to
3 had to
4 'm not allowed to

3 a

2 Abdullah said that he had already received his voting card.
3 Aileen said that she was voting by absentee ballot.
4 Zoe said she had never voted before.
5 Linda told Paul that she was going to vote for the party with the greenest policies.

3 b

1 Brian said he couldn't vote because he wasn't registered.
2 Jane said she thought she would watch the candidates' debate on TV.
3 The official said I wasn't allowed to wear my Labour Party badge in the polling station.
4 The official said they had to count the votes again.
5 The reporter said the new prime minister might give a speech soon.

A political speech

Alliteration: E
Euphemism: G
Exaggeration: C
Metaphor: A
Parallelism: H
Repetition: B
Irony: F
Rhetorical question: D

Stats & pics: The UK General Election 2019

1 They are pie charts.
2 The pie charts are taken from Statista. They were published in 2021.

3 Chart A gives an overview of the share of the UK vote in the 2019 general election. It is divided into five segments. Four of the segments represent four political parties while the fifth represents votes for other, smaller parties. The Conservatives received the largest share of the vote with 44%. The Labour Party were second with 32%. The Liberal Democrats had a 12% share while the Scottish National Party had 4%. Others got 9% of the vote.
Chart B shows how the seats in the House of Commons were divided after the 2019 election. It is divided into the same number of segments as Chart A and represents the share of seats for the same parties. The Conservatives make up a majority of the seats with 56%. The share for Labour is almost the same as their share of the vote at 31%. The Scottish National Party received 7% of the seats while the Liberal Democrats got only 2%. Others had 4% of the seats.

4 It can be concluded that the 'first-past-the-post' voting system in the UK does not usually give the same percentage of seats to a party as the share of the vote they win. Only the Labour Party has a similar share of seats to its share of the vote. I find it surprising that the Conservatives got 56% of the seats when they did not get a majority of the votes. The charts could serve as a wake-up call to British voters.

Writing workshop: Writing a comment

1

a Pro	c Pro	e Con	g Pro
b Con	d Pro	f Con	h Con

2 a

Democratic societies have a balance of freedoms and responsibilities: a
Politicians need votes to be elected: d
Let us look at the effect on election campaigns: c
Finally, it is worth noting how people feel about being 'forced' to vote: g
Looking at the other side of the argument, citizens of the UK and US do not seem to feel the enthusiasm for compulsory voting: b
Compulsory voting cannot be seen as a way to create a perfectly fair society: f
As for election campaigns, the drive to motivate voters to get out and vote is what makes campaigns exciting: h
Lastly, the balance between freedom and rights on the one hand and duties and responsibilities on the other is important: e

2 b

Democratic societies must be careful that politicians do not just do what benefits their voters: d

However, compulsory voting does not magically create equality: f

Election campaigns are an important part of the democratic process: c

That argument may ignore the risk that instead of more debate, there could be less: h

Let us look at how people feel about being 'forced' to vote: g

Australians may simply be happy with the system they are used to. British and American voters may feel the same: b

Finally, we should consider the balance of freedom and responsibilities in democracies: a

Yet we should consider what we mean when we talk about freedom: e

3

a 1 but, 2 Furthermore
b 3 because
c 4 In contrast
d 5 On the one hand, 6 On the other

Going deeper

1

a They married privately a couple of days before the larger royal wedding.
b The baby is/was a girl. The baby was due in/that summer.
c They tried (hard) to get more support from the palace/royal family.

2

c

3

Meghan E
The British monarchy D
The British tabloid press A

4

1 comparing, 1995
2 money, his mother
3 history, Meghan

Fun & games

1

The United Kingdom:
1 CONSERVATIVE PARTY
2 CONSTITUENCY
3 DEVOLUTION
4 HOUSE OF COMMONS
5 HOUSE OF LORDS
6 LABOUR PARTY
7 MONARCH
8 MP
9 PARLIAMENT
10 PRIME MINISTER

The United States:
1 CONGRESS
2 DEMOCRATIC PARTY
3 ELECTORAL COLLEGE
4 HOUSE OF REPRESENTATIVES
5 INAUGURATION
6 NATIONAL CONVENTION
7 PRESIDENT
8 REPUBLICAN PARTY
9 SENATE
10 STATE PRIMARY

2

1	chips	6	autumn
2	mobile	7	pavements
3	queue	8	biscuit
4	trousers	9	tram
5	toilets	10	holiday

3

1 kicked off
2 front-runner
3 own goal
4 knock-out punch
5 below the belt
6 sprint to the finish line
7 tight race
8 neck and neck

4

V O T E

Topic 4

Words in context

1 b

1 you take into account: B
2 I think we should: –
3 In my view: D
4 a meaning that I share: –
5 In my opinion, it is time: A
6 In conclusion, I believe: F
7 a conclusion I would draw: C
8 if you ask me: E

2 a

to exploit sb/sth: sich etw zunutze machen
to be addictive: süchtig machen
to arouse interest
to affect sb/sth: The Corona pandemic affected everyone all over the world.
to portray: darstellen
to advertise to sb
brand: OTHER COLLOCATIONS: leading/well-known/popular/top-selling/own brand, a brand of sth
to subscribe to sth
to publish: veröffentlichen

sensationalist: sensationslüstern
to manipulate sb/sth: Online games can manipulate children into spending real money.
rumour: I heard a rumour that Rob and Jennie were dating.
bias: Vorurteil, Einseitigkeit
report
to pose a risk

2 b

addictive	disinformation
disagree	repost
contentious	misleading
impressionable	socialize

2 c

The growing trend to spend more time online means that companies are using web marketing increasingly often. Clickbait posts with sensationalist headlines, contentious topics and controversial or familiar images have a much higher hit rate than other forms of marketing. When it is done correctly, this kind of advertising can capture the emotional needs of the viewers and drive them towards inspiring and relevant content.

2 d
1 to add fuel to the fire
2 to shut the stable door after the horse has bolted
3 to cotton on (to sth)

2 e

Children and fools speak the truth. – Proverb: Kindermund tut Wahrheit kund.
A storm in a teacup. – Idiom: ein Sturm im Wasserglas
To pour oil on troubled waters. – Unknown: die Wogen glätten
There are three kinds of lies: lies, damned lies, and statistics. – Benjamin Disraeli: Es gibt drei Arten von Lügen: Lügen, verdammte Lügen und Statistiken.
A lie can be halfway around the world before the truth gets its boots on. – Mark Twain: Eine Lüge ist bereits dreimal um die Erde gelaufen, bevor sich die Wahrheit die Schuhe anzieht.

Getting to grips with grammar

1
1 had to / would be
2 will I know / do
3 wouldn't have / didn't exist
4 hadn't done / would have invented
5 sees / 'll never talk
6 had deleted / wouldn't have damaged

2

used to be
used to visit
didn't use to phone

used to be
cost
didn't get
didn't use to feel
didn't use to have
didn't use to get
used to be

3 a
1 was preparing
2 was helping
3 was doing
4 were shopping
5 was lying
6 was writing
7 were working
8 weren't doing / were shooting

3 b
1 was crossing / happened
2 was listening / didn't hear
3 shut down / was uploading
4 saw / was texting
5 were waiting / arrived
6 was searching / found
7 grabbed / was talking
8 didn't notice / was looking

Stats & pics: Internet usage

1

The chart is taken from the JIM-Studie. It was published in 2021.

2
1 remained
2 reached
3 has gradually gone down
4 had fallen
5 are using
6 has risen

Writing workshop: Writing a summary

1

It's a feature article.

2

c, e, f, g, h

Mediation: A question of trust

2

circulation: Auflage
subscriptions: Abonnements
beliefs: Überzeugungen
recent: jüngste
to a certain extent: in gewissem Maße

distort: verzerren
sources: Quellen
bias: Voreingenommenheit
back up: belegen

3

1 The circulation of printed news has gone down by 50% / has halved in the last four decades.
2 She thinks that journalists in the traditional press are influenced by their beliefs and are not objective anymore. She thinks that certain subjects are not debated.
3 Forty per cent of Germans do not fully trust the media because they feel that the media, to a certain extent, distorts the truth and hides some facts.
4 She only trusts information which can be backed up – everything else she treats as opinion.

Going deeper

2

1b, 2c

3

Showing that you are open-minded: A, D
Asking questions: B, E

4

1 discover it ourselves
2 keep it short and simple
3 the original misinformation
4 add your own comments
5 we can protect

Fun & games

1

Emma Watson – Jane Goodall – Nelson Mandela – Harvey Milk – Greta Thunberg – Malala Yousafzai – Martin Luther King Jr. – Mahatma Gandhi

2

TikTok 2014   WhatsApp 2009
Twitter 2007   YouTube 2005
Facebook 2003   Snapchat 2011

3

1 Oh my god!
2 I don't know
3 let me know
4 rolling on the floor laughing
5 by the way
6 talk to you later
7 to be honest
8 be right back
9 in my opinion
10 laugh out loud
11 thank god it's Friday
12 in real life

4

New media:
ALGORITHM
ECHO chamber
EMOJIS
FOLLOWERS
SLACKTIVIST
TARGETED advertising
TEXT message

Traditional media:
MAGAZINE
NEWSPAPER
public service BROADCASTER
quality PRESS
radio STATION
TABLOID
TV PROGRAMME

Skills

Writing a comment

1 b

Balancing an argument with a counter argument: 7, 8, 9
Defining the topic: 1
Drawing a conclusion: 13, 15
Expressing a personal opinion: 2, 14
Giving arguments a logical order: 4, 5, 10, 11
Giving examples: 6, 12
Outlining what the writer is going to do: 3

Doing a creative writing task

1 b

a letter to a newspaper editor
the editor and the readers of the newspaper
formal
to give my opinion and share my experience

Analysing and describing charts and graphs

a

1 In a few years, the figures will have recovered to their value of 20...
2 From 20.. until 20.., the percentage remained relatively stable.
3 Over the last # year(s), figures have steadily increased.
4 The current trend shows the value of XYZ is increasing.
5 In the year 20.. the value of XYZ fell drastically to a low of #.
6 The percentage has not yet reached its previous high point.

b

The graph was published by Statista in 2021. It is a bar chart and it shows the estimated value of the tourism sector in New Zealand as a percentage share of the country's GDP. From 2010 until 2019, the tourism sector's share of GDP remained stable at 13–14%. In 2020, however, the GDP value of the sector fell drastically to a low of 6%. Between 2020 and 2021, it has/had recovered/risen by only one per cent, but the current trend shows its value is increasing. According to forecasts in the graph, by 2025 the tourism sector will have recovered to 13% of GDP – the same value as in 2014 and only one percentage point below its value in 2019, before the Covid-19 pandemic.

Presenting

b

talk – giving – make – finish – interrupt – turn – moving – discuss – look – expand – showing – summarize – remind – saying

Dealing with listening tasks

1 a

1 reasons – no trust – politics – US – local and federal level – politicians – laws – companies – influence – corruption – dishonesty – personal connection

2 government – build more trust – people affected – government – decision making – press conferences – journalists – normal citizens – live television – special ministry – choices – minorities – people of colour

1 b

1 reason/cause
trust/belief
politics/government
local/state
federal/national
politicians/representatives
laws/regulations
companies/businesses
influence/persuade
corruption/scandal
dishonesty/lies
personal connection / personal contact

2 government/administration
trust/confidence
people affected / stakeholders
government/authorities
decision making / choices
press conference / interview
journalists/reporters
normal citizens / regular people

live television / live TV
special ministry / special department
choices/decisions
minorities / ethnic groups
people of colour / Black people

1 c

Sentence 2: modal verb – a verb must follow / to be elected maybe you need to be famous / rich / have good ideas

Sentence 3: get the time + to-infinitive / the verb 'face' collocates with problems/issues/challenges and the verbs fix/solve/address also collocate with problems/issues/challenges

2 a

1 c, d; 2 a, c

2 b

will have more trust
be rich or get money from big companies
to think about solving the problems

2 c

Lindsey: A, D, F
Jamal: B, E, G

Using dictionaries

1 b

1 the legal right to vote in your country's elections
2 noun
3 /ˈfræntʃaɪz/
4 countable
5 formal
6 American English
7 ●○○

2 a

1 motions   4 tally
2 quorum   5 tie
3 clerk

2 b

2 quorum: the smallest number of people who must be present at a meeting so that official decisions can be made

3 clerk: an official in charge of the records of a court, town council etc

4 tally: a record of how much you have spent, won etc by a particular point in time

5 tie: the result of a game, competition, or election when two or more people or teams get the same number of points, votes etc

2 c

6	amendment	9	measure
7	impeached	10	objects/opposes
8	unanimous		

Stylistic devices

a

phrases you do not need: employs humour to make the point, Irony, Rhetorical Question

"Well, folks …": Informal register/tone

"This is a test …": repetition of the same sounds

"A 102-year-old woman …": makes the message more convincing

"… the example of America …": Parallelism

"the Capitol, …": makes the situation easier to picture

"America …": Personification

b

"They voted early. They voted absentee. They voted in person. They voted by mail. They voted by drop box."

By repeating a phrase, the speaker puts more emphasis on the points and makes it more memorable.

Describing and analysing cartoons and pictures

1 a

Chris Madden; the issue of how people can be affected by conspiracy theories which are spread on social media.

1 b

In the foreground, you can see <u>two men who are walking on a pavement towards the right of the cartoon</u>. In the background in the top left, corner, there is <u>a large sign</u> which says <u>"the truth" in big, capital letters and has an arrow pointing left</u>. The man in the centre seems to be <u>following the other</u>. The man in front is <u>not looking where he is going. Instead, he is staring at a smartphone</u>. A caption on the right shows us that <u>he is telling the man behind him to ignore the large sign. He also says that social media tells him that "the truth is a conspiracy theory" to keep people in their place</u>. The man behind is <u>looking at the large sign</u> and he seems to <u>be about to reach for the man in front</u>.

1 c

The point of the cartoon seems to be that social media is the source of a lot of conspiracy theories and that some social media users only believe what they want to hear on social media even when the truth, in big letters, is clear for everyone to see.

The caption is ironic in the sense that the first man seems strong because he orders the second man to

ignore "The Truth" – but he only does that because social media tells him what to think.

Furthermore, there is some humour in the fact that the man in front says social media tells him that "The Truth" is just a trick to keep him in his place and not think independently – in fact he doesn't think for himself.

The man following behind might actually be more independent because he is looking at "The Truth" and appears to be reaching towards the other man, maybe to stop him.

1 d

In my opinion, the cartoonist makes his point effectively because the cartoon uses humour. Although it is sometimes difficult to know what or who to believe on social media and people can be manipulated, I think the cartoonist is telling us to be responsible for deciding our own opinions and not to take our opinions from people on social media or others who say they know what 'the truth' is.

2 b

The picture is divided into two halves. The left-hand side has a light-yellow background. In the centre, there is a prominent image of a smartphone. The screen of the phone is dark blue and the body a darker shade of blue, almost black. The screen shows an image of a person, seen from the side. It looks like a man. He is wearing white shirt and light-brown trousers. It looks like he is sitting inside the phone. He is looking at another phone or tablet in their hands and it looks like a strip of paper is coming out of the phone and flowing out of the phone screen. Thin bars go from the top of the screen to the bottom. The phone looks like a window into a prison cell. All around the central image of the phone there are icons and symbols coloured red and white from mobile technology. These include a checklist in the top-left corner, a social media comment with a 'thumb-up' symbol at the top, a speech bubble with a heart in the top-right, an email symbol showing the number eight on the right of the phone, a red rectangular shape with the shape of a person in the bottom-left corner, a red circle with a white heart in its centre towards the right of the phone and finally a pair of speech bubbles with the number six on the left of the phone. The right-hand part of the image has a light blue background, and it features an image of countryside or a garden in pastel colours, green and turquoise leaves of plants and light green grass. There are three wavy clouds in the sky. The garden image has a curved, wavy outline, not straight or square. In the centre of the garden image, there is a lady sitting with her legs crossed. She is wearing a white T-shirt and a dark blue, almost black, skirt. The wind appears to be blowing her long, red hair to the left. She is holding a book and one of the pages seems to be turning. She appears to be looking out of the picture at the viewer.

2 c

The atmosphere in the left-hand side is very hectic and full of (digital) activity. The image of the man inside the phone conveys a feeling of being trapped. Although the social media symbols are positive: hearts and thumbs-up, the red colour suggests a warning. The right-hand side of the image forms a stark contrast with the left because the atmosphere is much calmer and more relaxed.

The left-hand side: Its atmosphere is achieved by the seven social media symbols surrounding the phone and the strip of 'paper' flowing out of the phone in the man's hands and out of the phone. The numbers on the symbols represent unread messages/emails and likes. The strip of 'paper' seems to represent the news feed of a social network home page. The darkness of the phone contrasts strongly with the lighter colour of the background. The image of the man sitting in the phone conveys a lack of freedom – the four 'walls' of the screen are very close to him while the bars suggest that he is trapped.

The right-hand side: Its atmosphere is achieved by the image of nature and the artist's use of light shades of greens and blues with no sharp contrasts in tone. The wavy outlines of the garden image and the wind blowing through the woman's hair suggest freedom and a much more relaxed state. Furthermore, there is no action taking place – it is simply a woman sitting on the grass and reading.

2 d

The image clearly illustrates the idea of the man on the left being trapped inside a social media 'prison', while the woman is outside in the fresh air relaxing with a book and enjoying her 'freedom'. I feel, however, that it is too simplistic and probably represents the opinion of someone who is opposed to modern digital technology. It is easy to depict life without technology as being 'freedom', but our society could not survive if we rejected technology like the artist seems to want us to do.

Analysing a text

1 a

The author is / The text was written by Priti Patel, the British Home Secretay. It appeared / It was published in The Telegraph on the 8th of September 2021.

1 b

a comment – argumentative – clear conclusions and demands

1 c

The author employs a formal register. This is indicated by complex sentence structures and vocabulary such as <u>conduct</u>, <u>despicable</u> and <u>misconception</u>.

1 d

serious – dramatic – warning – determined

1 e

1 A lot of child abuse happens on the internet. / Keeping the internet safe is not only a matter for governments and the police.
2 Increasing the privacy of social media apps could put children at greater risk. / Facebook should change its plan for end-to-end encryption.
3 More money needs to be spent by internet companies to protect people. / The UK wants to encourage firms to invent new ways of protecting young internet users.

1 f

1 factual data
2 directly addressing
3 metaphors
4 alliteration
5 repetition

b Write the names of the people from a) on page 4 beside the opinions.

1 This person thinks his/her parents' adolescence was just as hard for them as for teens today. _____

2 This person feels young people today have more freedom to be different and be individuals. _____

3 This person thinks that young people today need more psychological help to cope with stress. _____

4 This person believes that he/she has to work harder at school than his/her parents did. _____

2 a You can find the highlighted words from the text on page 4 in the table below.
Fill in the empty boxes in the following wordlist. In the 'Memory support' column you can either …
- put the word or phrase in a sentence, or
- think of words belonging to the same family, or
- write down other collocations.

Word/Phrase	Memory support	German
to **take an exam**	In Ireland, students in their final year take their state exams in June.	
to **nag sb**		jdm mit etw. in den Ohren liegen
to **live up to**	The team didn't live up to their fans' hopes and lost the final game.	
mature	Age is only a number; how you behave shows whether you are mature or not.	
to **have a baby**	I'm going to wait until I'm 30 before having any babies.	
	OTHER COLLOCATIONS: a challenge/difficulty/conflict	etw gegenüberstehen
peer pressure	Peer pressure can be positive, e.g. when friends stop someone from doing something they shouldn't.	
verbal abuse	Abuse can take many forms: verbal, physical, sexual and emotional.	
threat	WORD FAMILY to threaten sb (e.g. with violence) to make a threat threatening (adj)	
self-esteem		Selbstwertgefühl
compulsory		obligatorisch
vulnerable	Harry felt emotionally vulnerable after his dog died.	
	WORD FAMILY anxious (adj)	Besorgnis, Unruhe
independent	WORD FAMILY	unabhängig
authority figure	My parents are very relaxed: they don't believe in having too many rules and acting like authority figures.	

2 **b** Which words or phrases from the 'Words in context' article fit the situations below.

1 You shouldn't f_____ your p_____ alone, talk with parents or friends about them.

2 Mum always n_____ me to take off my shoes when I come home.

3 You should be proud of your acne – it shows you are becoming m_____.

4 Jane and Brendan split up, so Jane is feeling quite v_____ at the moment.

5 Daniel told his parents about the t_____ that were posted by bullies on his Facebook.

6 Brian: My older brother got top grades and was captain of the football team – I hate that my parents expect me to l_____ u_____ t_____ him.

7 Many parents said they felt p_____ p_____ to give their children smartphones earlier than they wanted to.

8 I don't need to post selfies and get 'likes' to boost my s_____-e_____: I'm happy with who I am.

c The verbs *have*, *get*, *take* collocate with other words to make many common English phrases. Complete the sentences with a form of *have*, *get*, or *take*.

1 The Covid-19 pandemic _____ a huge impact on people everywhere.

2 Teenagers, don't _____ on too many extra challenges – just being an adolescent is difficult enough.

3 Ms Ashdown won't be our teacher next year because she is going to _____ a baby.

4 I don't think I'll _____ married when I grow up.

5 I don't _____ along with my grandparents – their values are too different to mine.

6 When Paul turns 17, he is planning to _____ his driving test.

d If you can't think of a certain word, saying what it means can help. Find words in the 'Words in context' article to match these paraphrases.

1 It describes something that you have to do because it is the rule, e.g. kids have to go to school. _____

2 This is using words – written or spoken – to hurt other people. _____

3 This is the result of an action or a situation. _____

4 This verb means you feel the negative effects of something bad. _____

5 These are people in our lives who have power or control. _____

6 This word means the feeling of worry and stress. _____

e Write English paraphrases for these words from Topic 1.

1 approval _____

2 to meet a deadline _____

3 accomplishment _____

4 independence _____

5 community work _____

Getting to grips with grammar

Do after Sections C and E

1 Talking about the present: states and activities

You know that a verb like *have* is used in its progressive form to describe actions and in its simple form to describe states. Other verbs like this are: *look, think, see, sound*. Some verbs are normally used to describe states and not usually used in the progressive form: *believe, belong, forget, hate, imagine, know, like, love, mean, need, own, prefer, remember, seem, understand, want*.

G ▶ *simple present, present progressive, SB p. 163*

Three friends are starting a rock band. Complete their talk with the correct form of the present: simple or progressive.

Oliver: Hi Luke! Where's Kim?

Luke: She_____ (come). She_____ (put) her bike at the back of the house.

Kim: Hi Oliver! I_____ (look forward) to our first band practice today.

Oliver: Yeah, me too. But first, we _____ (need) a name for the band. _____ you _____ (have) any ideas?

Luke: Yeah – *The Fantastic Three*? What _____ you _____ (think)?

Oliver: It _____ (sound) like we're superheroes, not a rock band. How about *Three will rock you*?

Kim: Sorry, I _____ (not like) it. I _____ (prefer) something shorter. Hey, I _____ (know)! What about the first letters of our names? K – L – O.

Oliver: K – L – O or *klo*. I _____ (imagine) people would say it like a word. It _____ (seem) O – K, Kim. What _____ you _____ (look) at on your phone, Luke?

Luke: I_____ (do) a search for *klo*. I _____ (remember) it from school, but I _____ (forget) why. Oh! Ha, ha, ha.

Kim: Why _____ you _____ (laugh)? Show me. Oh, I _____ (see).

Luke: Oliver, *klo* _____ (mean) toilet in German. I _____ (not think) we _____ (want) to have a name like that.

Kim: No way. People will say our music is... Wait! I've got it! We take the first *two* letters of my name, K – I. *Kilo*!

Luke: *Kilo*! I _____ (love) it. *Kilo* play *heavy* rock, man!

G ▶ *The future,*
SB p. 166

2 Talking about the future: predictions using *will* and *going to*

> The choice between *will* and *going to* can depend on the words we use and the how the speaker sees a situation. We usually use *going to* when we know or see something *now* that tells us what can happen *soon*. We normally use *will* when we talk or give our opinion about a time further away in the future and with words like: *expect, hope, maybe, think, imagine.*

Complete the dialogues with the verbs and the *going to*-future for one part and the *will*-future for the other.

a Lydia: This summer, the weather hasn't been very nice. I hope it_____ (be) better for our

holiday next week.

Mum: So do I, Lydia. Look at those huge black clouds. It_____ (rain) again.

b Ibrahim: Oh no. Liverpool scored again! 2–1 and only 2 minutes left. They_____ (win).

Alan: Yeah, *this* game maybe. But I still think Manchester United _____ (win) the league.

c Matilda: Watch my new dance move for my TickTack video. This time maybe I_____ (get)

more *likes*.

Brian: That's cool. Hey, be careful! The flowerpot _____ (fall)!! Too late.

d David: Tom, look at Kevin. He's walking over to Mandy. OMG! He_____ (ask)

her to the disco!

Tom: He's crazy. She _____ (not say) yes; she never goes to discos and, anyway, she

likes Henry.

e Mae: Can you give me your phone charger? Quick! The battery is at 1 %. It _____

(turn off)!

Jennie: My charger is in my locker. It _____ too long to get it. Ask Jake. He always has

one in his pocket.

3 Articles: *a/an, the,* and no article

Trouble spots with articles: The rules for using *a/an, the,* or no article are very much like the rules in German, but there are some differences that can trip you up.

> *a* or *an*: We use *an* before words (singular nouns or adjectives + singular nouns) that begin with *a, e, i, o, u*. But some vowels are spoken like consonants: university, European, and *h* – a consonant – is sometimes silent: hour, honour.

a Complete the sentences with *a* or *an*.

1 Kevin asked _____ interesting question which

the teacher couldn't give _____ good answer to.

2 Frieda never wore _____ uniform to school until

she went on _____ exchange to Scotland.

3 Mum, do you have _____ hat? I need _____ old

hat for my Halloween costume.

4 Orla has been in the bathroom for _____ hour

and _____ half!

5 _____ 11-year-old boy was on TV because

he was the youngest student to go to _____

American university.

6 Linda wouldn't give me _____ honest

answer when I asked her if she had been

at _____ party.

G ▸ *The definite article, SB p.167*

the or no article: Talking about things in a general way. When we talk about home, school, university/college, hospital, prison or church *in a general way*, we do **not** use *the*.
It is the same with general concepts and ideas: *I love history; Prices are rising; People everywhere are talking about it; French and English share a lot of vocabulary.*
But when we are talking about a *specific building*, e.g. the church across the street, or *specific things*, e.g. The history of Ireland ...; The price of video games ...; The people in our street; The English spoken in Scotland... ; we do use *the*.
Be careful! We always use *the* with other places: *the cinema, the theatre, the bank, the mall/ shopping centre, the doctor/dentist, the station/airport, the city centre.*

b Complete the pairs of sentences with the given word. Use *the* if necessary.

1 school: In Germany, _____ begins before 8am, but in Ireland classes begin at 9am.

A lot of parents were waiting outside _____ to meet their children after the class trip.

2 hospital: I've never been very sick – I've never had to go to _____ .

The government wants to close _____ in our town.

3 prison: Sometimes I hear someone playing the piano in _____ near where I live.

In some countries people are sent to _____ just because they don't agree with their

government.

4 college: My older sister starts _____ next month in another city.

After my A-Levels, I want to study at _____ where my father studied.

c Yvonne is an American exchange student in Duisburg. She emails her friends. Complete her email with *the* where needed.

Hi everyone,

I can't believe that I've been here in _____ city of Duisburg for three weeks already. Time flies

when you're having _____ fun! My host family – _____ Brauns – are wonderful and my host sister,

Andrea, is really cool. Duisburgers are rather friendly – well, all _____ people I've met so far have

been friendly. My host parents actually come from Munich and _____ German they speak sounds

quite different to their children and to _____ accents in _____ books we study at _____ school in

_____ US. _____ one thing that's a bit hard is that _____ family eat _____ meat. You know that I

don't. But my host-mom has been super, and we go shopping for a lot of rice, pasta and

vegetables. Doing _____ family things together is really important to my host-family. Sunday is _____

day everyone does things together. Back home, we go to _____ mall on Sundays, but here, if _____

weather is nice, we go on an *Ausflug* (a trip) to _____ countryside, which is great because you

know I love _____ nature. I'm enjoying _____ school a lot but studying all of _____ school subjects

in German is much harder than I expected. What's _____ latest news from back home? Write and

tell me. Love, Yvonne.

Stats and pics: A question of faith

Do after Section B

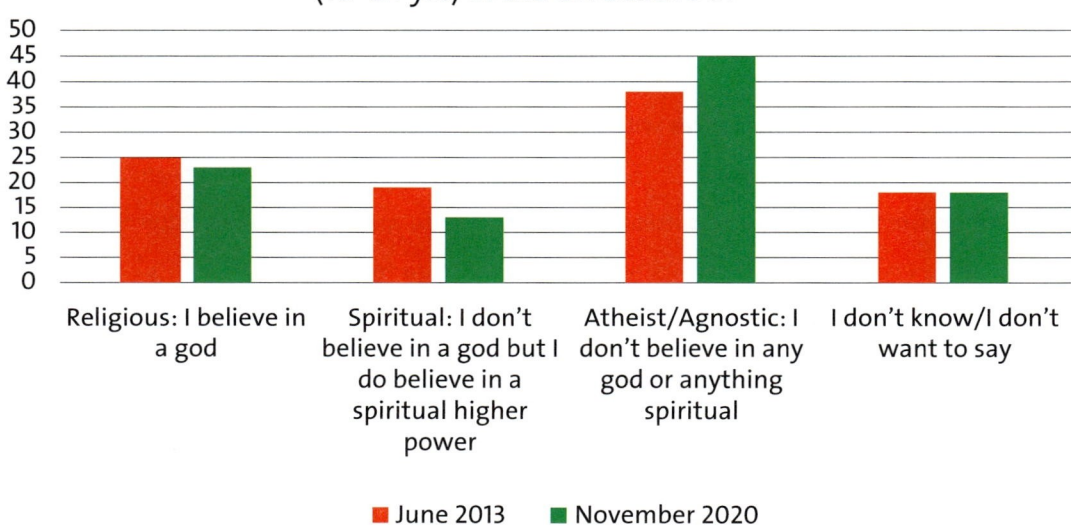

A question of faith: what do young people
(16–24 yrs) in the UK believe in

Religious: I believe in a god | Spiritual: I don't believe in a god but I do believe in a spiritual higher power | Atheist/Agnostic: I don't believe in any god or anything spiritual | I don't know/I don't want to say

■ June 2013　■ November 2020

1　What kind of diagram is it? _____

2　What does it show? _____

_____

3　Write some sentences for describing the changes in the groups between 2013 and 2020.

Use the words from the box. Use each one only once and change the form if needed.

between 2013 and 2020 | biggest | decrease | go down | grow | in the seven years | remain | slightly | the amount of | the number of | the figures for | the same

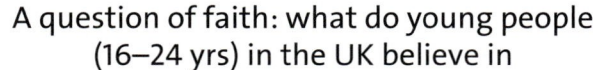

How to say or write it

Trends happening now, use the **present progressive:** *The number of electric cars on our roads* **is rising.** 　　G ▶ p. 163
When describing finished time periods in the past, use the **simple past:** *Between 2015 and 2020, the number of electric cars* **rose** *by 150 %.* 　　G ▶ p. 164
For time periods including the present, use the **present perfect:** *Recently, the number of electric cars* **has risen** *by a huge amount.* 　　G ▶ p. 164

4　What conclusion can you draw from the graph? _____

_____

Song

A Hero's Death

Life ain't always empty

Don't get stuck in the past
Say your favourite things at mass
Tell your mother that you love her
5 And go out of your way for others
Sit beneath a light that suits ya
And look forward to a brighter future

Life ain't always empty

Sink as far down as you can be pulled up
10 Happiness really ain't all about luck
Let your demeanour be your deep down self
And don't sacrifice your life for your health
When you speak, speak sincere
And believe me friend, everyone will hear

15 Life ain't always empty

Bring your own two cents
Never borrow them from someone else
Buy yourself a flower every hundredth hour
Throw your hair down from your lonely tower
20 And if, and if you find yourself in the family way
Give the kid more than what you got in your day

Life ain't always empty

Ah, never let a clock tell you what you got time for
It only goes around, goes around, goes around
25 Take your family name for your own great sins
'Cause each day is where it all begins
And don't give up too quick
You only get one line, you better make it stick
If we give ourselves to every breath
30 Then we're all in the running for a hero's death

Good to know

Fontaines D.C. – A punk rock band from Dubl n, Ireland. They came together because they all loved poetry.

The singer/songwriter, Grian Chatten, wrote this song as a letter from a father to his child, who he doesn't live with. Grian said when he wrote it, he was remembering times when he felt down and he wrote the song as a way of giving advice to someone feeling this way.

ain't [here] **isn't**
stuck *festgesteckt*
mass *Gottesdienst*
to **go out of your way for sb** *sich besonders anstrengen, etw. für jn zu tun*
to **suit sb** *jdm stehen*
demeanour *Benehmen*
sacrifice *opfern*
sincere *ehrlich*
to **(give/bring) your own two cents** *deinen eigenen Senf dazugeben*
to **borrow** *borgen*
to **be in the family way** *schwanger sein*
in your day *als du ein Kind warst/in deiner Kindheit*
sin *Sünde*
to **be in the running** *im Rennen sein*

1 Match these tips to a line or lines in the song.

  a Help people. Line _____

  b Act like who you really are. Line _____

  c Have your own opinion, don't let others
     make it for you. Lines _____

  d You only live once so you should make the
     most of it. Line _____

2 Find two more tips in the song and write them in your own words. Give line numbers.

  a _____

  b _____

3 Imagine you are the child. How does the letter make you feel? Better or worse? Give some reasons for your answer.

  _____

  _____

  _____

4 The song uses a rhyming style. Write your own two lines of 'advice for life' using a rhyming style.

  _____

  _____

Literature

Do after Section E

Radio Silence by Alice Osman is a novel about Frances Janvier, a 17-year-old mixed-race British girl. Frances has always been one of the best in her school and everybody expects her to go on to Cambridge University. But Frances also has a secret side: as a talented, anonymous artist who draws artwork for a very popular YouTube series. In this excerpt, Frances is taking part in an interview as part of her application to Cambridge University to study English Literature.

alongside *neben*
to **blink** *blinzeln*
to **nod** *nicken*
to **glance at sth.** *einen kurzen Blick auf etwas werfen*
disillusionment *Desillusionierung*
alienation *Entfremdung*
horrific *entsetzlich*
passionate *leidenschaftlich*
to **do a degree** *studieren*
to **encourage** *anregen*

I messaged Mum that I was going in and she messaged back saying she believed in me. I just wished I believed in me, to be honest. [...]

The two interviewers were both old white men. I'm sure that not all of the interviewers at the University of Cambridge are old white men, and in my second interview later that day one of them was a woman, but in my first interview, mine were old white men, and I was not surprised. They didn't offer to shake my hand, so I didn't offer either. My interview went a little bit like this. 5

OLD WHITE MAN (O.W.M.) #1: So, Frances, I see that you picked art A level alongside English, history and politics. And you did maths at ASLevel. Why such a diverse group of subjects?

FRANCES: Oh ... well, you know, I've always been interested in a wide range of subjects. I just thought, at A level, you know, it'd be good to, sort of, keep that going, you know, using both sides of 10 the brain, having a wider ... broader ... learning experience. I enjoy lots of different subjects, so, yeah.

O.W.M. #1: [blinks and nods]

O.W.M. #2: And you say in your personal statement that the book that really started your interest in the study of English literature was [glances at paper] The Catcher in the Rye by J.D. Salinger?

FRANCES: Yes! 15

O.W.M. #2: What was it, precisely, about the book that so inspired you?

FRANCES: [completely unprepared for a question like this] Ah ... yeah. Well, I think it was the themes, really, I really related to the themes of, you know, disillusionment and alienation, [laughs] you know, the typical teenage thing you go through! Erm, but yeah, there were lots of things in the book that really interested me from, like, an academic point of view, like, erm ... One of the things 20 I liked was the way Salinger sort of got the lingo of nineteen-forties and -fifties teenagers? It was the first time I'd read an old book – well, like, a classic book anyway – that, erm, you know, really felt like it had a real voice? I really felt connected to the main character, I guess ... and it made me want to understand why.

O.W.M. #2: [nods and smiles, but doesn't really seem to have heard anything I've just said] 25

O.W.M. #1: So, Frances, I suppose the big question is: why do you want to study English literature?

FRANCES: [horrific pause] Well ... [another horrific pause – why couldn't I think of anything to say?] Well, I-I've always loved English literature. [A third horrific pause. Come on. There are more reasons than that. It's fine. Take your time.] English literature has always been my favourite subject. [That's not true, is it?] I've been passionate about studying it at university since I was little. 30 [What absolute bullshit. You're going to have to sound less like a robot if you want them to believe you.] I love analysing texts and learning about their— their contexts. [I don't understand, why are you being like this? You sound like you're lying.] I think doing an English literature degree would encourage me to read a lot more than I do. [Wait, so you're saying you don't read lots already? Why are you applying to study English literature in the first place?] I think ... [Why are you applying to 35 study English literature at university?] I think I've always ... [Always what? Always been lying to yourself about this? Always believed that you were passionate about something you weren't?]

O.W.M. #2: Okay, well, let's move on.

(605 words)

1 Are the following statements true or false?

True   False

a Frances feels sure about herself before the interview. ☐ ☐

b She expected the interviewers to be more friendly. ☐ ☐

c The first interviewer (OWM #1) is interested in knowing why Frances studies
subjects that are very different from each other. ☐ ☐

d As part of her university application, Frances wrote a text describing why she
wants to study English Literature at Cambridge. ☐ ☐

e In the interview, she explains clearly how one novel began her love of English
literature. ☐ ☐

f Frances' inner voice helps her to stay calm and give good reasons why she
wants to study literature at Cambridge. ☐ ☐

2 Match the aspects of the writing style with the correct ending.

Aspects of the writing style

1 The author writes as if she were Frances.
This style of writing

2 A disadvantage of this style is that it

3 By writing the interview in the style of a
scripted dialogue,

4 By allowing us to hear Frances' inner
dialogue with herself, the author

Effect on the reader

A doesn't allow us to know what other
characters are really thinking.

B shows us the real meaning behind the
words Frances' says to the interviewers.

C lets us see everything from the main
character's point of view and is called
first-person narrator.

D we can easily follow the scene as if we
were watching a movie or play.

3 Read the lines given in the text and finish the sentences in your own words.

a (ll. 7–25) Old White Man #1 and #2 don't react to Frances' answers about her A Level subjects

and *The Catcher in the Rye* because her answers _____

_____

b (ll. 16–24) Frances was not prepared for her interview. You can see this in the text where _____

_____

c (ll. 27–37) Frances can't finish her answer to OWM #1's 'big question' because _____

_____

4 On the cover of the book it says, "Listen to your own voice". The novel is described as a YA –
Young Adult – novel. Now that you have read the text, what do you think 'Listen to your own
voice' means for young adults like you?

_____

_____

_____

5 You choose: a) Imagine you are Frances in the weeks after the interview. Write a short email to
your friend explaining what the result of the interview was and what you have decided to do.
OR b) Write a short dialogue between Frances and her mother when Frances arrives home.

Going deeper

Do after Section E

You are going to listen to a podcast where two young people talk about the issues which worry teenagers today.

Before you listen

Look at the list of issues that adolescents say they worry about.
How important are they to you? Rank them from 1, the most important, to 10, the least important.

☐ Climate change and the environment   ☐ Finding a good job after school/college

☐ Gun violence at school   ☐ Getting into college/

☐ Bullying   ☐ Being unfriended on social media

☐ Having a good social life   ☐ Family issues

☐ Getting good grades at school   ☐ Your health

🔊 As you listen
01

1 Tick the topics mentioned by Jennie and Chris

☐ Covid-19   ☐ Applying to college

☐ Negative stereotypes of teens   ☐ Climate change

☐ Youth unemployment   ☐ Alcohol and drugs

☐ Racism   ☐ Peer pressure

2 Choose the right answer. If necessary, listen again.

1 Jennie thinks that ...
  a older people never want to understand teenagers.
  b today's teenagers are harder for older people to understand.
  c it has always been difficult for some older people to understand younger people.

2 Chris feels that ...
  a there is peer pressure to join youth protests.
  b people who don't join youth protests are bad.
  c school strikes stop teenagers from getting good grades.

3 Jennie says young people should ...
  a try to be like Greta Thunberg.
  b take small steps to protect the environment.
  c stop their parents driving.

4 Chris thinks ...
  a finding a job is more important than protecting the planet.
  b being selfish is okay when you have a good job and money.
  c it is important to get a good start in his own life first.

3 Complete the sentences.

a In the United States, the number of adolescents suffering health problems due to anxiety and

low moods is _____ ten years ago.

b The problem of unemployed young people is _____ right now.

c Jennie and Chris _____ about some points, but they _____

with each other that young people who are feeling stressed should talk to someone.

Fun & games

Do after Topic 1

1 Guess who! → A question of identity

    a This poem describes someone from Topic 1 in your student's book. Complete each line with a word from the box. **TIP:** the first letter of each line spells the person's first name.

Big | Conservative | Equality | Healthy | Hip-hop | Jay-Z | One | Pop | Progressive | Rock | Said | Sia

_____ music fits their style,

_____ lie they wrote on their profile,

_____ they'll be a nurse, maybe they might,

_____, they believe, is everyone's right,

_____ describes their political beliefs,

_____ beats give their ears some relief!

    b Now it's your turn! Write your own poem describing yourself. Remember: Each line must begin with a letter from your name.

2 Lost in translation

Older people can have problems when it comes to understanding what adolescents say. Match the teen slang terms from the list with the correct definition. For the terms given in the table (which some German teens use), write your own English definitions.

bae | boots | ghost | lit | open crib | no cap | throw shade

Slang word(s)	Definition
_____	This means you're telling the truth and not lying.
_____	This means your parents are not at home and you can do what you want
cringe	
_____	your best friend; your girlfriend/boyfriend; someone who you think of before anyone else.
fresh	
_____	Exciting, excellent. It comes from how someone's face seems to light up when they see something amazing.
_____	To ignore somebody and act like they're not there; to suddenly stop all social media contact with somebody without explaining why
lost	
_____	To criticize somebody; to show that you don't like or disagree with somebody
_____	Used as an adverb in the same way as 'very' or 'a lot'

Good to know

Slang is adaptable and can change quickly in any language. The English language, however, is especially adaptable and is growing all the time. 5,400 new English words are 'created' every year and around 1,000 of those are added to dictionaries. A lot of these words come from young people, the internet and technology, other languages, and world events, e.g. the Covid-19 pandemic: social distancing, superspreader.

3 Crossword: Personality

Solve the crossword puzzle. Every word is an adjective which can describe somebody's personality.

Clues:

Across →
- **1** ernst
- **4** bizarr
- **7** entspannt
- **10** stur
- **11** empfindlich
- **14** ängstlich
- **16** leidenschaftlich

Down ↓
- **2** extrovertiert, kontaktfreudig
- **3** egoistisch
- **5** unehrlich
- **6** gescheit, vernünftig
- **8** zurückhaltend
- **9** spaßig
- **12** schlau
- **13** ruhig
- **15** mürrisch, launisch
- **17** dämlich, absurd, affig

Words in context

1 **a** Read the article on Dublin, Ireland's capital city.

The place where you ==grow up== is part of your identity, and Dubliners, just like Londoners or Berliners, have their own particular character too. You will probably hear them call the city 'Dirty old Dublin' with their typical black humour. Nobel Prize winner
5 James Joyce even wrote a book of short stories about them in 1914.

A lot of time has passed since Joyce, but some things never change: the love-hate relationship between the North and South sides of Dublin, for example. The capital of Ireland, divided by the river Liffey, lies on the east coast of Ireland looking out onto the Irish sea.

10 In Dublin's north ==inner city==, you are more likely to find highdensity, council-built apartment complexes, where the ==closeknit communities have long been plagued== by crime and drugdealing, alongside tiny, terraced bungalows built in the 1940s. Rents on this side of the city, while still high by European stan-
15 dards, are lower than in the south, though ==gentrification== and long-delayed renovation of public housing means prices are

==catching up==. In Dublin's south inner city, you will find the upmarket high-rise buildings housing luxury hotels and the European headquarters of some of the world's leading multinationals.

The North-South divide can also be seen in the greater Dublin area. Detached and semi-detached
20 houses with well-tended gardens are much more common in the southside's leafy ==suburbs==. Public ==amenities== here are in better supply and well maintained. The lovely sandy beaches on the coast and mountains and lush ==rural== areas to the south are the main reason why ==property== has always been more expensive here. In contrast, the northside's suburbs have large, sprawling council estates, more rundown areas, many industrial estates, and Ireland's largest airport.

25 Dublin doesn't have boroughs or districts like other cities. Instead, areas are named after the original villages which were swallowed up by the growing city. It has a numerical system – the areas north of the Liffey are odd-numbered: Dublin 1, 3, 5, etc. and in the south even.

30 One thing that unites North and Southsiders is Dublin's ==public transport==. The city relies on a fleet of notoriously unpunctual buses, only two tram lines (which ==serve== the southside more than the north) and no underground rail system – despite thirty years of promises. These problems, combined with the narrow streets typical of older European cities, make Dublin city centre's severe ==congestion== the second
35 worst in Europe, after Moscow. Over the last twenty years, the pressure of rising prices has led to the commuter belt around Dublin becoming ever wider, with former city dwellers moving out to buy cheaper homes and get on the 'property ladder', despite the long ==commute== to work.

(445 words)

b Are the following sentences true or false? Correct the false ones.

1 Not everything about Dublin has changed since James Joyce's time.

2 There is very little development in Dublin's north inner city.

3 In the past, Dublin had a lot of smaller towns around it.

4 Dubliners disagree about its public transport system.

5 More and more Dubliners are moving out of the city to find jobs in other places.

to **grow up** *aufwachsen*

love-hate relationship *Hassliebe*

high-density *dicht bebaut*

council-built *Sozialbau-*

close-knit community *sehr enge Gemeinschaft*

to **be plagued by sth** *von etw geplagt sein*

terraced (house) *Reihenhaus*

gentrification *Gentrifizierung*

public housing *Sozialwohnungen*

to **catch up with sth/sb** *jdn/etw einholen*

high-rise building *Hochhaus*

upmarket *exklusiv*

to **house sb/sth** *jdn/etw beherbergen*

suburb *Vorstadt*

detached house *Einfamilienhaus*

semi-detached house *Doppelhaushälfte*

amenity *Einrichtung*

rural *ländlich*

lush *saftig*

sprawling *ausgedehnt*

property *Immobilie*

council estate *Siedlung mit Sozialwohnungen*

rundown *verwahrlost*

industrial estate *Gewerbegebiet*

borough *Stadtteil*

to **swallow sth (up)** *etw verschlingen*

numerical *zahlenmäßig*

to **rely on sth/sb** *sich auf jdn/etw verlassen*

fleet *Flotte*

notorious *berüchtigt*

to **serve sth/sb** *jdm/etw dienen*

congestion *Stauung*

commuter belt *Einzugsgebiet*

property ladder *Immobilienleiter*

to **commute** *pendeln*

2 **a** You can find the highlighted words from the text on page 17 in the table below.
Fill in the empty boxes. In the 'Memory support' column you can …
- put the word or phrase in a sentence, or
- think of words belonging to the same family, or, write down other collocations.

Word/Phrase	Memory support	German
to **grow up**	I grew up in an apartment in the city, so I had to share my bedroom with my brother.	
inner city	**WORD FAMILY** inner city (n) inner-city (adj)	
close-knit community		sehr enge Gemeinschaft
	OTHER COLLOCATIONS: unemployment, anti-social behaviour, vandalism	von etw geplagt
gentrification	**WORD FAMILY** to gentrify (v) gentrified (adj)	
to **catch up with sb/ sth**	Although the number of electric vehicles on our streets is growing, it will be a long time before their numbers catch up with traditional petrol cars.	
	WORD FAMILY suburbia (n) suburban (adj)	Vorstadt
amenity	Our village is growing and needs more amenities especially for our children – a swimming pool and a sport centre, for example.	
rural		ländlich
to **commute**	**WORD FAMILY** commuter (n) commute (n) commuter (adj)	
	OTHER COLLOCATIONS: ~ ladder, ~ owner, ~ investor, private ~, public ~	Immobilie, Liegenschaft
accent	The London accent is very different from the accent of people from the north of England.	
public transport		öffentliche Verkehrsmittel
to **serve**	New York is served by three major airports: John F Kennedy, LaGuardia, and Newark.	
congestion	Traffic and people cause congestion – for example, shoppers at Christmas fill our city centre streets.	

2 b Find four pairs of opposites in the ten words from 'Words in context'. Write them in the table. There are two words you do not need.

commute detached divide

property rundown rural

terraced unite urban

well-maintained

....

....

....

c Match the two halves of the sentences and highlight the phrases from 'Words in context'.

1 Getting your foot on the property

2 House prices in Toronto's commuter

3 Crime has always

4 Holiday makers love the lush

5 An accident caused severe

6 Graffitti artists chose a new upmarket

a plagued cities, just like honey attracts flies.

b hotel on main street for their latest 'artwork'.

c congestion on the M1 motorway this morning.

d belt have risen by 20% in the last five years.

e ladder is harder for young people today.

f rural landscapes in the British Lake District.

d Pronounce these words from 'Words in context', writing down the correct spelling.

1 [ɪnˈdʌstrɪəl ɪsˈteɪt] ....

2 [ˈsʌbɜːb] ....

3 [ˈpʌblɪk ˈhaʊzɪŋ] ....

4 [ˈhaɪraɪz] .... - ....

5 [ˈvɪlɪdʒ] ....

6 [ˈkʌntrɪˌsaɪd] ....

7 [ˈkæpɪtl] ....

8 [ˈbʌrə] ....

e Without looking at SB pp. 61–62, write the answers to these questions.
What do you call ...

1 ... a day when the people celebrate their country?

....

2 ... the native people who belong to a particular place or region and didn't come from somewhere else?

....

3 ... a place that is so pretty you would like to take a photo of it?

....

4 ... attractive natural features of a landscape, such as mountains, rivers and forests?

....

5 ... the time and activity when powerful, rich countries controlled other poorer countries?

....

6 ... the traditional accepted way of acting in a society or country?

....

Getting to grips with grammar

Do after Sections B and E

G ► *The simple past, SB p. 164, the present perfect, SB p. 164*

1 Talking about past events: with and without present effects

> We use the **simple past** to talk about completed actions in the past. Signal words include *when, yesterday, last week/month/year, in the past* and *ago*.
> We use the **present perfect** for situations that started in the past but continue until the present or affect the present. Signal words are *how long, this morning/week/year, recently, ever, yet, since* + date (e.g. *since 1990*) and *for* + period of time (e.g. *for two years*).

Complete this article about gentrification with the verbs in the simple past or present perfect.

Phibsboro is a district of Dublin. Bad Boys Café _____ (open) three years ago on the main street. "We _____ (be) busy since day one," says the manager, "and nobody complains that we are part of gentrification." Long-time Phibsboro resident Gillian agrees. "It's not a problem if somebody turns a shop that _____ (close down) years ago and _____ (be) empty for ten years into a hipster cafe. But look at the big developers. They _____ (buy) a lot of land here recently and since then _____ (knock down) many of the old buildings." Gillian and other local inhabitants who _____ (live) in Phibsboro for generations are angry. "The noisy construction work _____ (make) our lives hell," Robert tells me. He shows me a large apartment building next to his small house. "The developers _____ (build) that two years ago and since the day they _____ (finish) it, the sun _____ (not shine) on my house or garden for longer than an hour a day," he says. His doctor thinks this _____ (affect) Robert's health. "I _____ (be) always healthy until those developers _____ (move in). But this year I _____ (already miss) weeks at work because of illness."

G ► *Comparisons, SB p. 174*

2 Making comparisons

> We use *-er (than) / the -est* with one-syllable adjectives, e.g. *small – smaller – the smallest*. For two-syllable adjectives ending in *-y*, the *-y* changes to *-i*, e.g. *easy – easier – the easiest*.
> We use *more / the most* with adjectives of two or more syllables, e.g. *important – more important – the most important*.
> We compare two people/things with *than*, e.g. *London is **more expensive than** Berlin*.
> We use *(not) as … as* to say how things are (not) the same, e.g. *Berlin is **not as big as** London*.
> Note the irregular forms: *good – better – best; bad – worse – worst; far – further – furthest*.

Complete the sentences to compare Baden-Württemberg, Ireland and New Zealand. Use the correct comparative form of the adjectives given. You can get help on the internet.

In terms of land area, Ireland is _____ **(large)** Baden-Württemberg but _____ **(small)** New Zealand.

In terms of population, Baden-Württemberg has _____ **(big)** population while Ireland's is _____ **(big)** New Zealand's.

B-W is _____ **(sunny)** Ireland but New Zealand is _____ **(sunny)**.

The cost of living in New Zealand is _____ **(high)** in Baden-Württemberg, but Ireland is _____ **(expensive)** place to live.

3 Asking questions

> **Closed questions** have *yes/no* or short answers e.g. *Did you take the train? – Yes, I did.*
> We usually form them in the following way:
> auxiliary (form of *do/have/be* or modal verb) + subject + main verb (infinitive / *-ing* form / past participle)
> *Do you speak English?* • *Is John studying?* • *Have you seen Patrick?*
> <u>Exception</u>: *be* as the main verb, e.g. *Is Coventry a nice city?* • *Was the train clean?*

a Complete the closed questions with the correct form of the auxiliary and main verbs.
   TIP: The short answers can help you.

1 _____ you _____ (know) Canberra was the capital of Australia?
   – No, I didn't.

2 _____ you ever _____ (take) the London Underground?
   – Yes, I have.

3 _____ Dublin _____ (have) a high crime rate?
   – No, it doesn't.

4 _____ they _____ (build) a new sports centre here?
   – Yes, they are.

5 _____ rental costs _____ (rise) in Auckland over the last five years?
   – Yes, they have.

6 _____ Sydney _____ (introduce) a congestion charge? – Yes, it should.

> **Tag questions** can be used to make small talk more engaging.
> We form them with an auxiliary verb + subject pronoun. If the (auxiliary) verb is positive, the auxiliary in the tag question is negative, and the other way around.
> *You like Dublin, don't you?* • *You didn't study there, did you?*
> We use tag questions with a falling intonation to confirm what we think is true.
> We use tag questions with a rising intonation to ask real questions.

b Complete these tag-questions with the correct form of the auxiliary and a subject pronoun.

1 Newcastle is in the north-east of England, _____?

2 Tracy hasn't done her presentation yet, _____?

3 The police arrested the graffiti artist, _____?

4 People don't speak English in Quebec, _____?

> **Open questions** must be answered with more information.
> They start with a question word, e.g. *What (kind/sort of), Where, When, Who, Which, Why, How (much/many/long/far)*.
> **!** If we want to know who does/did an action, then we form the question without *do/does/did*.
> **Who** *lives in that house?* • **Which architect** <u>*designed*</u> *the Seattle Space Needle?*

c Ask open questions about the underlined information.

1 Canberra became the capital of Australia <u>in 1913</u>.

_____

2 <u>Half a million</u> people live in Dublin.

_____

3 They are building <u>a sport centre</u>.

_____

4 A short-journey ticket on the London Underground costs <u>£5.50</u>.

_____

5 Wellington is in <u>New Zealand</u>.

_____

6 <u>Banksy</u> painted that graffiti.

_____

Song

Do after Section B

gold rush
Goldrausch

wrecking ball
Abrisskugel

lath and plaster
Putzträger und Putz

condo
Eigentumswohnung

haunt *Lieblings-*
platz, Treffpunkt,
Schlupfwinkel

to **take flight**
flüchten

to **replace** *ersetzen*

construction site
Baustelle

stranger *Fremder*

greater good
Allgemeinwohl

requiem
Totengedächtnis

skyline
Stadtsilhouette

dive *Bumskneipe*

to **sweep away**
wegfegen

crane *Kran*

to **devour**
verschlingen

to **ascribe**
zuschreiben

faith *Vertrauen*

to **sift** *durchgehen*

wreckage pile
Trümmerhaufen

rubble *Trümmer*

Gold Rush

Digging for gold in my neighborhood
Where all the old buildings stood
And they keep digging it down and down
So that the cars can live underground
The swinging of a wrecking ball   5
Through these lath and plaster walls
Is letting all the shadows free
The ones I wish still followed me
Followed me, followed me
(Please don't change)   10
(Stay) Followed me, followed me
(Stay the same)
I remember a winter's night
We kissed beneath the street lamp light
Outside a bar near the record store   15
That have been condos for a year and more
Now that our haunts have taken flight
And been replaced with construction sites
Oh, how I feel like a stranger here
Searching for something that's disappeared   20
Digging for gold in my neighborhood
For what they say is the greater good
But all I see is a long goodbye
A requiem for a skyline
It seems I never stopped losing you   25
Because every dive becomes something new
And all our ghosts get swept away

Deathcab for Cutie are an indie rock band from Seattle. The lead singer Benjamin Gibbard has lived in the Capitol Hill district of Seattle for 25 years and wrote this song because, he says, "As I've gotten older, I've become acutely aware of how I connect my memories to my geography and [how] the landscape of the city changes." (NPR.com)

It didn't used to be this way
Be this way, be this way
(Please don't change)   30
(Stay) Be this way, be this way
(Stay the same)
(Cranes) Be this way, be this way
(Devour the light)
(Strange) Be this way, be this way   35
(Appetite)
I've ascribed these monuments
A false sense of permanence
I've placed faith in geography
To hold you in my memory   40
I'm sifting through these wreckage piles
Through the rubble of bricks and wires
Looking for something I'll never find
Looking for something I'll never find

(44 lines)

Good to know

Songs are very much like poems with music. Song writers often make use of metaphors and similes in their lyrics. A **metaphor** uses words and imagery in a different context to their normal meaning, e.g. *gold rush* in this song. A **simile** compares something to something else, e.g. *life is **like** a box of chocolates*, and uses words such as *like, than* and *as*.

1 Give three examples from the lyrics of how "the landscape of the city" has changed.

_____

_____

_____

2 The song speaks about people digging for gold and at the end the singer is searching through wreckage piles. What do you think he means by 'something I'll never find'?

_____

_____

3 Do you think the singer has positive, negative or mixed feelings about the effects of the 'gold rush' on his neighbourhood? Give three examples of the imagery used in the song in your answer.

_____

_____

_____

_____

Writing workshop

Do after Section C

Formal and informal language

1 Read the article about a teenager's campaign to save his local skate park.

Local boy on a mission to save neighbourhood skate park

Seán Keogh, 17, has a mission: to save his local skate park from demolition. The park is under threat due to plans by developers Greenfield Ltd to construct an apartment complex on the site. When we enquired about the skate park, the developers informed us that their plans will provide facili-
5 ties for neighbourhood children. However, the project details we obtained from the district council only mention a playground for very young children and the skate park doesn't appear anywhere. Seán thinks the area does not require another playground: "There are already five in our area for little kids, that's more than enough. But for us teenagers there's only
10 the skate park. So if they trash it, we won't have *anywhere* to chill. There's nothing else in the neighbourhood for guys my age." What is Seán's plan? "I want every teenager in the area to email this guy Declan Flynn, the head of planning in the district council, to ask for the skate park to be protected. If enough of us speak out, he can't ignore us."

(13 lines)

2 Are the following statements true or false? Tick the correct options. Correct the false ones.

	True	False
1 The developers are going to build a centre for young people who live in the area.	☐	☐
2 The author of the article received the development plans from the developer.	☐	☐
3 Seán thinks that there are already too many playgrounds for younger children in the neighbourhood.	☐	☐
4 The skate park is the only leisure facility in the district for teenagers.	☐	☐
5 Seán wants every local teenager to email the developer to ask them to save the skate park.	☐	☐

3 Formal and informal vocabulary. Look at the underlined words in the text in exercise 1. Complete the table by matching the underlined items with words that have a similar meaning.

More formal	More informal	More formal	More informal
_____	ask (about sth)	relax	_____
request	_____	_____	say sth about sth
_____	build	_____	need
_____	get	demolish	_____
_____	give	would like	_____
people	_____	will not	_____
		consequently	_____

4 **Connectives. Complete the sentences describing causes and effects with the correct connective.**

although | a result of | consequently | due to | leading to | nevertheless | result in

1 The skate park is at risk of demolition as _____ the developer's plans to build a new apartment building.

2 The loss of this facility will _____ teenagers having nowhere to spend their free time.

3 When teenagers have nothing positive to do, they could turn to negative activities,

   _____ an increase in anti-social behaviour.

4 _____ the developers say they have considered children in their plans, they have only thought about very young children, not teenagers..

5 We have asked the developers many times to change their plans. _____, they have ignored us.

6 _____, we have decided to use 'people power' to try to save our skate park.

7 _____ public pressure, the local council might try to influence the developer.

5 **Look at the email Seán wants to send to Declan Flynn, the head of planning at the district council. The style he has used is too informal.**

Look back over exercises 3 and 4 and pages 59-60 in your student's book. Rewrite the email in a more formal way.

💾 ↻ ↺			− ☐ ✕

➤	To	
Send	Subject:	Please protect our skate park

Hi Declan,

_____

I'm writing to ask that you protect our local skate park.

_____

Greenfield Ltd wanna trash the park and build apartments on it.

_____

The park's given teenagers a place to meet and chill for years.

_____

Young guys like me aren't gonna have anywhere to spend our free time.

_____

Greenfield got permission from you for their plans.

_____

So, we want you to change that permission so that Greenfield'll have to keep the skate park or build a new one.

_____

_____

Best regards,

Seán Keogh

Stats & pics: Talking about cartoons

Do after Section E

Describing a cartoon

Each sentence describing the cartoon has <u>one</u> mistake. Cross out the mistake and write in the correct word(s) from the list.

look | map | background | ~~black and white~~ |

caption | depicts | in | countryside

"Which trail has the best cell-phone reception?"

    black and white
1 This ~~colourful~~ cartoon shows a scene from a national park.

2 In the distant foreground, you can see mountains.

3 The cartoon describes three people: a young couple and a man.

4 The young couple are looking as if they are at a nightclub because she has nice hair, earrings and a handbag.

5 The other man on the cartoon has just passed the couple and is now walking towards the right.

6 He is prepared for a walk in the nature because he is wearing a hat and a rucksack with a bottle of water.

7 The younger man is looking at a card and doesn't even notice the signpost or the park information.

8 There is a speech bubble below the cartoon.

Interpreting a cartoon

Match the beginnings of the sentences with the correct endings below.

1 The cartoonist is making • **2** The cartoonist • **3** The point the cartoon is making • **4** The artist is criticizing the behaviour

… is ridiculing people who go to the countryside but cannot relax and enjoy it.
… of those who worry about their phone signal instead of enjoying nature.
… a sarcastic comment on the behaviour of city people who visit the countryside.
… seems to be that that we are not able to take a break from our electronic devices.

Giving your opinion

Complete the sentence in your words.

In my opinion, the cartoonist is successful/unsuccessful in his/her portrayal of modern society because _

Going deeper

Do after Section C
You are going to listen to a news report about how London is trying to deal with traffic congestion.

Before you listen

carrot-and-stick policy *Politik von Zuckerbrot und Peitsche*

Authorities often use a 'carrot-and-stick' policy to change people's behaviour. Look at the measures below. Put either a 'C' in the box for a measure that encourages and allows a behaviour and an 'S' if it discourages or prevents it.

☐ congestion charges   ☐ fines and penalties

☐ traffic calming   ☐ banning motor vehicles from streets

☐ cheap public transport   ☐ park and ride schemes

☐ cycle lanes   ☐ low-emission zones

🔊 As you listen
02

1 Tick the correct answer (a, b, c, or d). There is only one correct answer.

1 An LTN is …
- **a** … an area where cars are completely forbidden. ☐
- **b** … a light transport network for residents. ☐
- **c** … an area where only people who live there can drive. ☐
- **d** … an area where only long car journeys are allowed. ☐

2 In December, angry Hackney residents …
- **a** … demonstrated against the plan by driving slowly to the town hall. ☐
- **b** … blocked the way to the town hall by parking their cars. ☐
- **c** … marched from their district to the town hall. ☐
- **d** … drove slowly from the town hall to their district as a protest. ☐

2 Match the opinions A–E to the headings. There are two for each group and one opinion that you don't need.

A healthier areas can mean higher house prices   **B** drivers shouldn't control all the streets

C gentrification is not all bad **D** some people will lose their jobs **E** the plans are anti-driver

Protesters think …   **The city council thinks …**

_____   _____

3 Complete the sentences.

1 People who live in LTNs _____ to and from home, but the journey may be _____ .

2 Forty-eight per cent of car journeys in London are _____ two kilometres.

3 People in Hackney are afraid that emergency vehicles will take _____ to reach accidents in LTNs.

4 Surveys show that a _____ of people living in London support measures to _____ pollution.

5 Seven out of ten households in Hackney _____ a car.

Fun & games

Do after Topic 2

1 Joining adjectives with a hyphen

a When you describe nouns, two words can be joined with a hyphen (-) to create a single adjective.

The word snake contains nine pairs of words that describe nouns.

TIP: Each adjective/noun combination appears in 'Words in context' on p. 17.

builtclosecouncildelayed**density**detachedhatehighknitlonglovenumberedoddrisesemitendedwellhigh

Example: *high-density* apartment complexes

_____	area	_____	garden
_____	apartment complex	_____	house
_____	building	_____	relationship
_____	community	_____	renovation

2 A presentation puzzle

a Complete the word puzzle. The missing words are from the presentation phrases on p. 48 of your student's book.

I'm happy to ... so many of you here today! (number 5)

If you have any questions during the walk, please don't _____ to interrupt me. (number 1)

I'd like to start by _____ ... (number 2)

OK, let me _____ by saying that ... (number 4)

Now we'll _____ on to ... (number 8)

Let's now _____ at ... (number 7)

The next _____ shows ... (number 9)

In this _____ we can see ... (number 3)

I would like to _____ with ... (number 6)

b When you have completed the puzzle, use the letters in the highlighted boxes to fill in the missing word.

You've been a great _____!

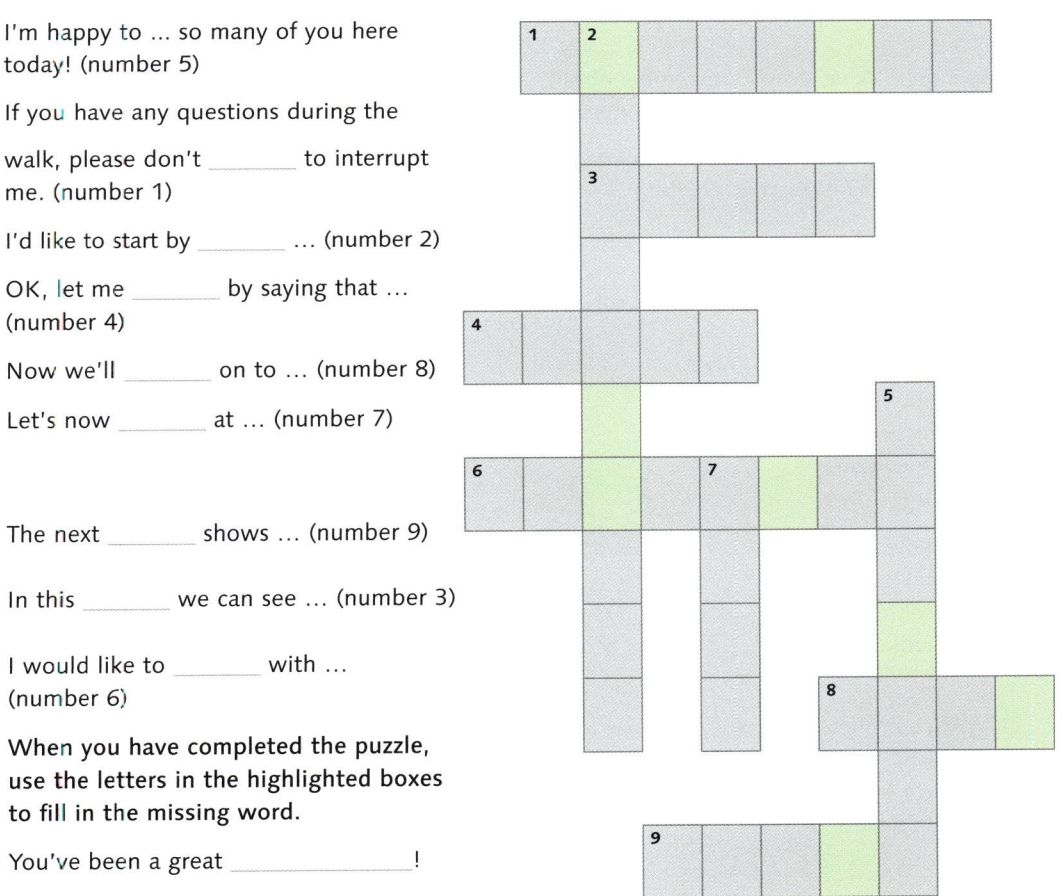

3 English idioms and sayings

Complete the sayings with a word from the box. Then match the meanings of 1-6 to the definitions a)–f) below.

door | home | house | kitchen | roof | wall

1 I hope Uncle Vernon isn't going to stay with us much longer. He's *eating us out of house and* _____.

2 Dad always packs too much for our camping trips. He takes *everything but the* _____ *sink!*

3 Before you criticize me, I think you should *put your own* _____ *in order*.

4 Tom thought Jane would say no to moving in together, but when he asked her, it was like *knocking on an open* _____.

5 When Jane came home late, her parents *hit the* _____.

6 My little brother asks questions all the time: it sometimes *drives me up the* _____.

____ **a** To become very angry		____ **b** To deal with your own issues before you talk about other people's problems
____ **c** Almost anything you can think of, even if it's not needed		____ **d** When something is much easier than expected
____ **e** To become annoyed by something, especially when it happens often		____ **f** To use a lot of somebody else's resources

4 Topic quiz: What do you remember about Topic 2 in your student's book?

a Mark or highlight the right answers and the letter. You need the letters in part b.

1 An expensive neighbourhood in London famous for its creative, artistic residents.
  – Notting Hill   S
  – Shoreditch   A
  – Kensington   E

2 A nickname some people have given Seattle.
  – Amageddon   U
  – Apocolypsia   D
  – Apple Town   E

3 The adjective 'affluent' is a synonym for
  – intelligent   I
  – wealthy   C
  – affordable   A

4 Which of these should you not say in English?
  – drive by car   K
  – ride a moped   T
  – go by bus   N

5 A name given to activists trying to improve safety for cyclists.
  – vigilante cyclists   B
  – wheeled warriors   T
  – guerilla cyclists   L

6 What kind of animal can you not find in New Zealand?
  – poisonous snakes   A
  – sheep   U
  – fur seals   L

7 Which famous series of movies was filmed in New Zealand?
  – Iron Man 1-3   R
  – the Jurassic Park movies   E
  – The Lord of the Rings   N

8 The poem which appears at the end of Topic 2 is called:
  – Rural America   G
  – Hometown   D
  – Clementine   H

b Write the letters after your answers in a. If your answers are correct, you will have the name of a city mentioned in Topic 2.

Words in context

1 **a** Read the text on young people and voting.

Young voters are often criticized because their <mark>turnout</mark> in past <mark>elections</mark> has been under 50%. As each new election comes around, people talk of the younger generation coming out to make their voices heard at the <mark>polling station</mark>. But when the votes are <mark>tallied</mark>, and the outcome analysed, young voters are still the age group with the lowest participation rates. We asked <mark>eligible</mark> young
5   voters to email and tell us why they *didn't vote* in the last election.

A In the UK, we've had the Conservatives and Labour for a hundred years. In America, they've had the Republicans and the Democrats forever. They're all the same and my vote won't change the result. So why should I bother to vote?

B I don't vote because there are no candidates my age. Our local MP visited our
10 school when he was <mark>campaigning</mark> in the <mark>constituency</mark> a couple of years ago. He was an old guy and spent more time talking to the teachers than us. Typical!

C Vote? Why? It's our politicians who made the world the way it is. They don't <mark>represent</mark> me. I go on demonstrations instead. Taking over the streets and marching for equality and to save the planet – that's real people power.

D To be honest, I don't know if I'm registered to vote – or how
15 to <mark>register</mark>. It seems complicated.

E I'm from Texas, but I go to college out of state – in New Mexico. So that means for elections during my college term, I need to apply for an absentee <mark>ballot</mark> to vote in my home state. Last time, I applied for one, but they changed the rules
20 and rejected my application. It's like they don't want me to vote!

How can we encourage more young people to vote? One way could be to say that 10% of election candidates should be aged between 18 and 30 to match their proportion of the population (only 3% of UK MPs are in that age group). More young people might vote if more of their peers <mark>stand for election</mark>. Apathy is a more difficult challenge and attempts to convince the young why they
25 should bother to vote have not made much progress. Is it time to follow Australia's example and make voting compulsory? Automatic voter registration on everyone's 18th birthday would help <mark>overcome the obstacle</mark> of complicated enrolment processes. <mark>Disenfranchisement</mark> through unfair rules and requirements is a risk any citizen can face, regardless of age, gender or race. The best defence is a free press and fair legal system so that the right to vote is protected. Active and moti-
30 vated citizens should of course be able to <mark>exercise</mark> 'people power' on our streets in a free society, but we cannot allow this to become 'mob rule'. This energy can be used productively if we make our political systems more responsive, e.g. more power to elected local government and a wider use of <mark>referenda</mark> for questions that affect our local and national communities.

(497 words)

b Note down the solutions the text suggests for the issues mentioned by the speakers A–E.

---

voter *Wähler/-in*
turnout *Wahlbeteiligung*
vote *Abstimmung, Wahl, Stimme*
to **tally** *Stimmen auszählen*
outcome *Ergebnis*
participation rate *Beteiligungsquote*
eligible *wahlberechtigt*
to **bother** *sich die Mühe machen*
MP *britischer Abgeordneter (Member of Parliament)*
to **campaign** *Wahlkampf machen*
to **register to vote** *sich zur Wahl anmelden*
to **apply for sth** *etw beantragen*
absentee ballot *Briefwahl*
to **reject sb/sth** *jdn/etw ablehnen*
to **encourage** *ermutigen*
peer *Gleichaltriger*
to **stand for election** *sich zur Wahl stellen*
apathy *Apathie, Gleichgültigkeit*
to **follow sb's example** *jds Beispiel folgen*
compulsory *verpflichtend*
to **overcome sth** *etw bewältigen*
obstacle *Hindernis*
enrolment *Registrierung*
disenfranchisement *Wahlrechtsentzug*
requirement *Voraussetzung*
to **face a risk** *sich ein Risiko gegenübersehen*
regardless of sth *ohne Berücksichtigung etw*
defence *Schutz, Verteidigung*
to **exercise (power)** *etw in Anspruch nehmen*
mob rule *Herrschaft der Straße*
to **affect** *betreffen*
community *Gemeinschaft*

2 **a** You can find the highlighted words from the text in the table below.
Fill in the empty boxes. In the 'Memory support' column you can …
- put the word or phrase in a sentence, or
- think of words belonging to the same family, or
- write down other collocations.

Word/Phrase	Memory support	German
turnout	The nice weather on voting day meant turnout was especially high.	
election	**WORD FAMILY**	Wahl, Abstimmung
	In the US this is also known as a polling place.	Wahllokal
to **tally**	Officials are tallying the votes right now and the results should be known in a few hours.	
eligible	In Scotland, young people from the age of 16 are eligible to vote in elections for the Scottish parliament, but the minimum age for UK elections is still 18.	
	The US has federal elections every two years, so it seems politicians never stop campaigning.	Wahlkampf führen
constituency	In the UK, one MP is elected for each of the 650 constituencies and each constituency has approximately 70,000 voters.	
to **represent sth/sb**	**WORD FAMILY**	jdn/etw vertreten
	WORD FAMILY register (n) registration (n)	anmelden
(an absentee) ballot	**OTHER COLLOCATIONS:** to be on the ballot the ballot box a spoiled ballot, a secret ballot	
to **stand for election**		(für eine Wahl) kandidieren
	OTHER COLLOCATIONS: ~ difficulties, problems, challenges, hurdles, resistance	ein Hindernis bewältigen
disenfranchisement	**WORD FAMILY** to (dis)enfranchise (v) franchise (n) (dis)enfranchisement (n)	
	OTHER COLLOCATIONS: to ~ your (democratic) rights to ~ caution to ~ an option	'die Macht des Volkes' ausüben
referendum, referenda (pl)	The full effects of the Brexit referendum in June 2016 have still yet to be seen.	

b Which words or phrases from 'Words in context' fit in the situations below? The lines show the number of letters.

1 Due to an agreement between the UK and Ireland, citizens from each country living in the other

are e___ ___ ___ ___ ___ ___ to vote in national e___ ___ ___ ___ ___ ___ ___ ___ in the country they

live in.

2 Some people feel voting on paper b___ ___ ___ ___ ___ ___ is more secure than voting on electronic machines.

3 I'm not interested in politics – I don't even know who r___ ___ ___ ___ ___ ___ ___ ___ ___ my

c___ ___ ___ ___ ___ ___ ___ ___ ___ ___ ___!

4 To have more women in parliament, 50% of the candidates who s___ ___ ___ ___ f___ ___

e___ ___ ___ ___ ___ ___ should be female.

5 People in Britain can r___ ___ ___ ___ ___ ___ ___ online to vote.

c Which words from 'Words in context' are described below?

1 The building where you vote in the United Kingdom: _____

2 One of the 650 people in the House of Commons in Westminster: _____

3 The name given to the total number of voters who actually vote: _____

4 Another word for result: _____

5 The process of taking away the right to vote from a person or group: _____

6 This means to count and is often used in the context of counting votes: _____

7 A yes/no vote on an issue in which all the voters of a country or state can take

part: _____

d Can you remember?

1 The names of the three branches of the US government are given in brackets, but the letters are mixed up. Without looking at section C of your student's book, can you write them correctly?

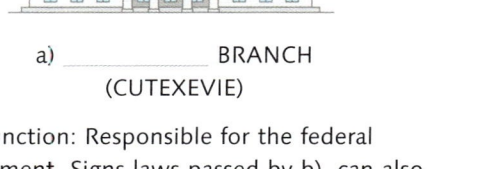

a) _____ BRANCH
(CUTEXEVIE)

Function: Responsible for the federal government. Signs laws passed by b), can also veto them. Can nominate judges to c).

b) _____ BRANCH
(GIVESTEAILL)

Function: Has the 'power of the purse', can pass laws. Can approve or reject judges nominated to c) by a).

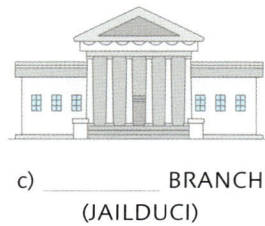

c) _____ BRANCH
(JAILDUCI)

Function: Checks that laws passed by b) and signed by a) are in line with the constitution. Oversees the federal and state legal system.

Getting to grips with grammar

Do after sections C and E

G ► The passive,
SB p. 170

1 The passive

> We use the **passive** to focus on an action or its results. We may not know who does the action or it is not important. The passive is often used in formal writing because it is indirect and less personal. We form the passive like this:
> Subject + a form of *be* + 3rd form of the main verb
> We can say who did the action by adding 'by + person', never '*from*'.
> **!** Some verbs do not have a passive form: *happen, occur, go, arrive, die, fall, stay*.

Complete the text with the passive form of the verbs in brackets. Use *by* if needed.

US Presidential elections take place every four years. They _____ (**must, hold**) on

the day after the first Monday of November in an election year. Presidents _____

(**not elect**) the people directly. Instead, the winner _____ (**decide**) the electoral

college. An American President cannot just do what he or she likes. Any decisions which cost

money _____ (**have to, approve**) Congress. Any law that _____

(**pass**) Congress _____ (**must, sign**) the President. If a President breaks the law, he

or she _____ (**can, remove**) Congress. This _____ (**call**) impeachment.

Donald Trump _____ (**impeach**) twice, but each time it _____ (**not

support**) the US Senate and he _____ (**find**) not guilty.

G ► Modal verbs,
SB pp. 166–167

2 Modal verbs

> **Modal verbs** do not change their form and, apart from *could*, only have present or, in some cases, future meanings. We use them to express concepts such as ability (*can*), obligation (*must*), permission (*can*, *may*), prohibition/lack of permission (*mustn't*, *may not*, *cannot/can't*), possibility (*can*, *could*, *may*, *might*, *would*) and lack of necessity (*needn't*).
> **!** There is no past form of *must* – we use *had to* instead.
> **Modal substitutes** can be used in all tenses and can express similar concepts: ability (*be able to*), obligation (*have to*, *need to*), lack of obligation (*not have to*, *not need to*), permission (*be allowed to*).

Use modal substitutes to express the same meaning as the highlighted words in the sentence before.

1 Official: Excuse me, sir. Your child may not go into the polling booth with you.

Child: I _____ go into the polling booth with Dad when he voted.

2 Official: If you register for a postal vote, you can vote even if you are out of the country.

Ben: I've registered. So even when I move to France, I _____ vote in the next election.

3 Daniel: Oh no! I must go home again to get my ID card.

Earlier today, Daniel _____ go home to get his ID card so that he could vote.

4 Official: The results are so close, we are counting again. The result cannot be announced, yet.

Reporter: I'm afraid I _____ tell you the results until the votes have been recounted.

3 Reporting what people say

G ▸ *Reported speech, SB pp. 168–170*

> When we report what people say, we use **reported speech**. *Say* and *tell* are the most common verbs to report speech. Other examples: *answer, claim, complain, mention, remind, warn*, etc.
> When we report what somebody said in the past, we usually change (or backshift) the tense.
> "Politicians *don't keep* their promises". → She said politicians *didn't keep* their promises. (simple present → simple past)
> "I *voted*." → He said he *had voted*. (simple past → past perfect)
> We normally change references to time in the same way.
> Ed: "I'm going to vote <u>tomorrow</u>." → Last week, Ed said he was going to vote <u>the next day</u>.
> If someone talks about something which is still true when we report it, or it is always true, we do not need to backshift.
> Expert: "Turnout in older groups *tends* to be higher than younger groups."
> The expert claimed that turnout in older groups *tends* to be higher than younger groups.
> **Careful!** The verb *tell* is followed by an indirect object, e.g He told *me* …

a Rewrite the sentences in reported speech, changing the tenses.

1 (Last Friday) Jamal: "I registered to vote yesterday."

Last Friday, Jamal said that he had registered to vote the day before / on Thursday.

2 Abdullah: "I have already received my voting card."

_____

3 Aileen: "I'm voting by absentee ballot."

_____

4 Zoe: "I've never voted before."

_____

5 Linda to Paul: "I'm going to vote for the party with the greenest policies."

_____

> **Modal verbs** can also change in reported speech.
> "I *can't* decide who to vote for." → He said he *couldn't* decide who to vote for.
> "New voters *must* register before 31 May." → She said new voters *had to* register before 31 May.
> "The polling station *may* still be open." → Joe told me the polling station *might* still be open.
> "The results *will* be shown live on TV." → Jo said the results *would* be shown live on TV.
> "You *mustn't* sit here." → The official told a man he *wasn't allowed to* sit there.

b Rewrite the sentences in reported speech, changing tenses and modal verbs.

1 Brian: "I can't vote because I'm not registered."

Brian said he couldn't vote because he wasn't registered.

2 Jane: "I think I'll watch the candidates' debate on TV."

_____

3 Official: "You mustn't wear your Labour Party badge in the polling station."

_____

4 Official: "We must count the votes again."

_____

5 Reporter: "The new prime minister may give a speech soon."

_____

A political speech

Do after section B

Read extracts from a speech by President Joe Biden in July 2021 on the subject of voting rights.

Look at your student's book p. 108 for more help.

Good to know

"**We the People**" are the opening words of the constitution of the United States. The constitution was created in **Philadelphia** at the Constitutional Convention in 1787.

Jim Crow refers to what is known as the *Jim Crow laws*. These were racist and discriminatory laws passed and enforced in the southern states of the US from the 19th century up until 1965. As well as making rules about where and what Black people could do, they also included rules about voting rights which meant many Black people could not vote.

Well, folks, good afternoon. There's a serious subject I'd like to talk about today. I'm here in Philadelphia at the National Constitution Center – the city and the place where the **A** story of "We the People" began. It's a story that's neither **B** simple nor straightforward. [...] But some things in America should be simple and straightforward.

Perhaps the most important of those things – the most fundamental of those things – is the right 5
to vote. The right to vote freely. [...] **C** With it, anything is possible. Without it, nothing – nothing. And for our democracy [to work], it's up to all of us to protect that right. [...]

Just think about the past election. A 102-year-old woman in Arkansas who voted for the first time on the very spot [where] she once picked cotton. A 94-year-old woman in Michigan who voted early and in person in her 72nd consecutive election. **D** You know what she said? She said this 10
election was, quote, "the most important vote that we ever had." [...] And the parents who voted for [the] school their children will learn in. Sons and daughters voted for the planet they're going to live on. Young people just turning 18 and everyone who, for the first time in their lives, thought they could truly make a difference. America and Americans of every background voted. They voted for good jobs and higher wages. They voted for racial equity and justice. They voted to make 15
healthcare a right, not a privilege. [...]

In fact, the fact that so many election officials across the country made it easier and safer for them to be able to vote in the middle of a pandemic was remarkable. As a result, in 2020, more people voted in America than ever in the history of America, in the middle of a once-in-a-century pandemic.

All told, more than 150 million Americans of every age, of every race, of every background exer- 20
cised their right to vote. They voted early. They voted absentee. They voted in person. They voted by mail. They voted by drop box. And then they got their families and friends to go out and vote. [...]

This should be celebrated – the example of America at its best. But instead, we continue to see an example of human nature at its worst – something darker and more sinister. In America, if you lose, you 25
accept the results. You follow the Constitution. You try again. You don't call facts "fake" and then try to bring down the American experiment just because you're unhappy. That's not statesmanship. That's not **E** statesmanship; that's selfishness. **F** That's not democracy; it's the denial of the right to vote.

[...] The **G** 21st century Jim Crow assault is real. It's unrelenting, and we're going to challenge it vigorously. 30

While this broad assault against voting rights is not unprecedented, it's taking on a new and, literally, pernicious forms *[sic]*. It's no longer just about who gets to vote or making it easier for eligible voters to vote. It's about who gets to count the vote – who gets to count whether or not your vote counted at all *[sic]*.

[...] To me, this is simple: This is election subversion. It's the most dangerous threat to voting and 35
the integrity of free and fair elections in our history. Never before have they decided who gets to count what votes count.

[...] [But] there's good news. It doesn't have to be this way ... We just need to show the will – the will to save and strengthen our democracy. [...] It requires us to unite in common purpose, to declare here and now: **H** We, the people, will never give up. We will not give in. We will overcome. 40
We will do it together. And guaranteeing the right to vote, ensuring every vote is counted has always been the most patriotic thing we can do.

(803 words)

In lines 25–27, Biden directly addresses his audience by using 'you', a common stylistic technique in political speeches. Match the highlighted lines A–H in the speech with these stylistic techniques. Look at p. 108 in your student's book for help.

| Alliteration | ____ | Parallelism | ____ | Euphemism | ____ | Repetition | ____ |
| Exaggeration | ____ | Irony | ____ | Metaphor | *A* | Rhetorical question | ____ |

Stats & pics: The UK general election 2019

Do after Section E

35

Chart A: Share of the UK vote % **Chart B: Share of seats in the House of Commons**

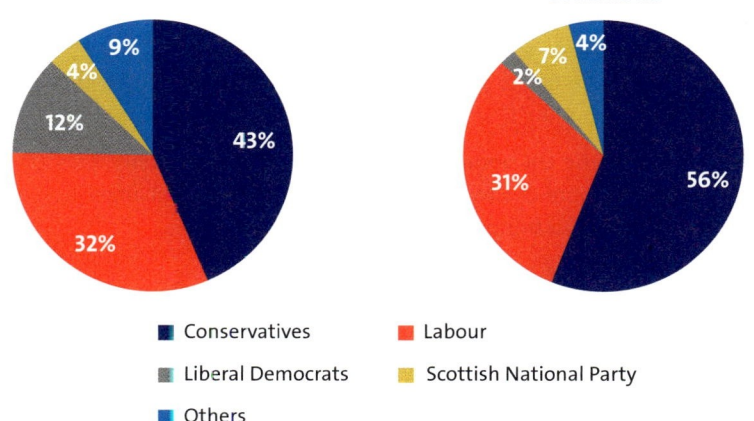

- ■ Conservatives
- ■ Labour
- ■ Liberal Democrats
- ■ Scottish National Party
- ■ Others

Source: Statista 2021

1 What kind of diagram are the two charts? _____

2 Where are the charts taken from and when were they published?

_____

3 Describe what the each chart shows.

Chart A _____

_____

_____

_____

_____

Chart B _____

_____

_____

_____

How to say or write it
The chart was published by … in … The chart on the left/right gives an overview of … It is divided into … segments/sections … Each segment represents … The … received the largest percentage/ share … while … The share for … is almost the same as … It can be concluded that … I find it surprising that … The charts could serve as a wake-up call …

4 Now analyse what a comparison of the two charts shows. What conclusions can you draw?

What surprises you about the charts?

_____

_____

_____

_____

Writing workshop: Writing a comment

The issue of compulsory voting was mentioned in 'Words in context' on page 29. In Australia, voting has been compulsory since 1924.

1 Look at the statements below and decide if they are best used to support compulsory voting (pro) or to argue against it (con).

a Voting can be seen not just as a right but as a civic responsibility. As such all citizens must do it – in the same way as everyone has to pay taxes and all children must attend _____ school.

b When given an opportunity to change the UK voting system in a 2011 referendum, people rejected it by a large majority. There is also no movement in the US to change _____ their system. Therefore, there is no need to bring in compulsory voting.

c In voluntary systems, political parties spend a lot of time and resources during campaigns trying to motivate people to vote. With compulsory voting, however, there is no need for political parties to do that, so there is a greater focus on the important _____ issues and policies of the parties.

d In a voluntary system, wealthier and older people vote in higher numbers than younger and poor people. That means politicians think more about the needs of the _____ wealthier and older people, and that can lead to an unequal society.

e The right to vote is a right all citizens have in a free and democratic country – being free also means being free to choose not to exercise your right to vote. _____

f Knowing that everyone has to vote does not necessarily mean that politicians will consider the needs of everyone. In Australia, even after 100 years of compulsory _____ voting, society is still just as unequal as in countries where voting is voluntary.

g Opinion polls in Australia regularly show that three-quarters of voters are happy with their compulsory voting system and do not feel it is a violation of their freedom. _____

h Compulsory voting could mean political parties stop trying to get people interested and engaged because they know people will have to vote anyway. _____

Look at your student's book p. 36 for more help.

2 Structuring the arguments in a comment. Look again at the points a) – h) in exercise 1.

a Place points a) – h) in the correct places in the body of a comment which summarises the supporting comments together first and follows this with the counter arguments (*Sanduhr-Methode*).

PRO	Democratic societies have a balance of freedoms and responsibilities. *a*
	Politicians need votes to be elected. ___
	Let us look at the effect on election campaigns. ___
	Finally, it is worth noting how people feel about being 'forced' to vote. ___
CONTRA	Looking at the other side of the argument, citizens of the UK and US do not seem to feel the enthusiasm for compulsory voting. ___
	Compulsory voting cannot be seen as a way to create a perfectly fair society. ___
	As for election campaigns, the drive to motivate voters to get out and vote is what makes campaigns exciting. ___
	Lastly, the balance between freedom and rights on the one hand and duties and responsibilities on the other is important. ___

b Place points a) – h) in the correct places in the body of a comment which follows each supporting comment with the counter argument (*Zick-Zack-Methode*).

Look at your student's book p. 36 for more help.

PRO	Democratic societies must be careful that politicians do not just do what benefits their voters. *d*
CONTRA	However, compulsory voting does not magically create equality. ___
PRO	Election campaigns are an important part of the democratic process. ___
CONTRA	That argument may ignore the risk that instead of more debate, there could be less. ___
PRO	Let us look at how people feel about being 'forced' to vote. ___
CONTRA	Australians may simply be happy with the system they are used to. British and American voters may feel the same. ___
PRO	Finally, we should consider the balance of freedom and responsibilities in democracies. ___
CONTRA	Yet we should consider what we mean when we talk about freedom. ___

3 Connectives. Complete the sentences below with the correct connective word(s) or phrases from the box.

because | but | furthermore | in contrast | on the one hand | on the other

a Democracies are meant to be free societies, 1 _____ forcing people to vote takes away their freedom to choose. 2 _____, in countries where only two parties dominate, how democratic is it to make people vote for candidates they may not even like?

b When voting is compulsory, the newly elected government is more legitimate 3 _____ it was elected by a true majority of the voters.

c In countries where voting is voluntary, turnout is usually around 66%. 4 _____, the average turnout in Australian elections is 94%.

d 5 _____, the percentage of Australian voters who deliberately ruin their votes in protest at compulsory voting is very small – only 5%. 6 _____, that small number of unhappy voters might decide the result in close elections.

4 You choose a) or b).

a Write your own comment, including an introduction and a conclusion, on the issue of compulsory voting. You can use the ideas from the exercises above and/or add your own.

or

b Write a comment on the issue of lowering the voting age to 16. You will have to research the topic yourself. An internet search using 'Scotland' and/or 'Wales' with key words '16' and 'voting age' will provide information on the topic in those countries.

Look at your student's book pages 104–105 and the PagePlayer App for more help.

Going deeper

Do after Section F

You are going to listen to a radio host, Ari Shapiro, ask Linda Holmes, of NPR, about the interview Meghan and Harry took part in with Oprah Winfrey.

🔊 **1** While you listen to part one, take notes on the following
03 points. You need not write complete sentences.

a Before Meghan and Harry's large royal wedding

_____

b The baby Meghan was expecting at that time

_____

c What Meghan and Harry tried to do about media harassment

_____

2 While you listen to part one, again find the correct answer (a, b, c, or d). There is only one correct answer.

a Meghan and Harry said …

    a that he had asked his family how they would feel if Meghan and Harry's baby had dark skin. ☐

    b the royal family were dealing with the racism Meghan experienced, but it was not enough. ☐

    c the royal family were making the racism problem faced by Meghan more difficult. ☐

    d the royal family were responsible for Meghan's mental health problems. ☐

🔊 **3** While you listen to part two, match the information A–E to the headings. There are two more
04 options than you need.

A controls the royal family through fear   **B** doesn't have many staff   **C** signed a contract with Harry

D is like a workplace which has a negative effect on your mental health   **E** was compared unfairly with Kate

Meghan	The British monarchy	The British tabloid press
_____	_____	_____

4 While listening to part two, again complete the sentences.

1 People are _____ the Oprah interview to an interview Princess Diana did

in _____.

2 Harry told Oprah that he does not receive _____ any longer from his family and he only

has what _____ left him.

3 Harry is afraid of _____ repeating itself: he does not want what happened to his mother

to happen to _____.

Fun & games

Do after Topic 3

1 British or American?

In the centre column you will find twenty features of the British or American political systems. Write the ter items which belong to the British political system in the left-hand column and the ten items belonging to the US political system in the right-hand column.

The United Kingdom		The United States
	CONGRESS CONSTITUENCY MP	
1 _____	DEMOCRATIC PARTY SENATE	1 _____
2 _____	MONARCH INAUGURATION	2 _____
3 _____	ELECTORAL COLLEGE LABOUR	3 _____
4 _____	PARTY HOUSE OF LORDS NATIONAL	4 _____
5 _____	CONVENTION HOUSE OF	5 _____
6 _____	REPRESENTATIVES HOUSE OF	6 _____
7 _____	COMMONS PRIME MINISTER	7 _____
8 _____	DEVOLUTION PRESIDENT	8 _____
9 _____	CONSERVATIVE PARTY REPUBLICAN	9 _____
10 _____	PARTY STATE PRIMARY	10 _____
	PARLIAMENT	

2 Lost in translation

The UK and the US share the same language, but there are sometimes differences in everyday vocabulary. Help the British man understand his American friend by writing the correct British English words from the box to match the American words in blue.

autumn | biscuit | chips | holiday | mobile | pavements | queue | toilets | tram | trousers

I beg your pardon, do you mean …

1 Man, I'd love some fries!   1 _____

2 Have you seen my cell phone?   2 _____

3 I don't like to wait in line.   3 _____

4 Do you like my new pants?   4 _____

5 Where is the restroom?   5 _____

6 My favourite season is fall.   6 _____

7 London sidewalks are too narrow. 7 _____

8 Would you like a cookie?   8 _____

9 I go to work by streetcar.   9 _____

10 I can't wait for my vacation!   10 _____

3 Politics is a contact sport
Elections and political campaigns are contests between politicians and parties, so you will often read or hear people use metaphors from the world of sport to describe them. Complete sentences 1–8 with the correct phrases from the four sports in the boxes.

• neck and neck • front-runner	• sprint to the finish line • tight race	• knock-out punch • below the belt	• own goal • kick off (v)

1 The presidential campaign _____ yesterday with the beginning of the first state primaries.

2 The young senator from Philadelphia is the _____ in the race to be the Democratic candidate after winning the support of the most states.

3 The Labour Party leader scored an _____ when she said the Tory leader was too young to be prime minister because he is only two years younger than she is.

4 The _____ in the general election seems to have been the promise by the Conservatives not to raise taxes – after that victory was certain.

5 In the debate between the presidential candidates, many people believe the Republican's joke about the Democratic candidate's children was _____.

6 Political candidates are campaigning hard in this final week as all the parties _____ of this general election.

7 There are only one or two percentage points between the candidates in opinion polls, proving this presidential election has really been a _____.

8 With the Conservatives and Labour having the same number of seats so far and only a few votes left to count – the parties are _____.

4 Topic quiz: What do you remember about Topic 3 in your student's book?
a Mark or highlight the right answers and the letter. You need the letters in part b).

   1 What was the average voter turnout in US presidential elections over the last 50 years?
   - 62%   D
   - 52%   S
   - 42%   V

   2 How often do presidential elections in the US take place?
   - Every 5 years   A
   - Every 4 years   O
   - When the president decides   E

   3 Unlike the US, the UK does not have a ...
   - written constitution.   T
   - a border with another country.   P
   - a monarchy.   E

   4 What name is given to the British system of deciding the winner of a constituency election?
   - First past the post   E
   - Proportional representation   I
   - Electoral college   Y

b Write the letters after your answers in a). If your answers are correct, you will know one of the best things you can do if you want a better world.

_____

Words in context

1 **a** Read the letter to a newspaper.

Dear Sir or Madam,

I was interested to read your article on the benefits of social media for young
people. But I am afraid I have to disagree with the author. -----A----- to treat
social media like tobacco and ban it for under-eighteens. You might think
that is shutting the stable door after the horse has bolted, but it is never too
5 late to do the right thing.

Social media exploits teens' need to be included and accepted by their peers, and its platforms are
addictive. Its algorithms choose content to arouse users' interest, 'likes' provide affirmation, while
fear of missing out works to keep people *always* online and up to date. Psychologists say these
stimuli affect the brain in biochemical ways and, -----B----- that teenage brains are still developing,
10 teens are more at risk of becoming social media junkies. US teens spend six hours a day online!
That means fewer chances to socialize face-to-face, less physical exercise and poorer mental health.

So-called 'influencers' with their curated photos and vain videos portray artificial, perfect lives.
They boast of their beauty, their luxurious lifestyles and wealth. At the same time, they earn their
living by advertising to impressionable teenagers. Our young people are bombarded with product
15 placement, brands and repetitive commands to *like*, *subscribe* and, above all, *buy*. So are these 'influencers' a positive influence on our young? That is not -----C----- .

Nearly half of all young people get their news from social media. -----D-----, that is very worrying.
Websites hungry for 'hits' publish misleading 'news reports' using 'clickbait' headlines with sensationalist language. Young people are often unable to recognise legitimate sources of news be-
20 cause they have less life experience. They can be manipulated into believing rumours and repost-
ing misinformation.

Due to the fact that we mostly connect with people who agree with us, social media acts like an
echo chamber. This prevents us from seeing our own bias and makes constructive debate more
25 difficult -----E-----. When disagreements happen online over contentious issues, impulsive teens
can lose control of their language and make offensive or defamatory comments, even post hate
speech. And what is posted online *stays* online. And that can have real world consequences: look
at the many reports of teens getting into trouble for their online behaviour or people losing jobs
in later life for abusive comments or opinions they tweeted as teens.

30 The teenage years are difficult enough already, but social media adds fuel to the fire. Take cyberbul-
lying, for example. As it happens on teens' handheld devices, it can reach its victims *everywhere at
any time*. Technology has made parenting harder than before – that is what 60 per cent of parents
say, and one in three admits arguing over screen time with their teens *every day*.

It took 60 years for us to cotton on to the dangers of smoking and ban it for under-eighteens. The
35 social media era is two decades old and the risks it poses to our teens' health and well-being are clear
as day. -----F----- we must not wait another 40 years before we do the right thing.

(516 words)

b Decide which of the phrases below can fill the six gaps in the text. Write the letter beside the
phrase. There are two you do not need.

1	when you take into account	____	**5**	In my opinion, it is time	____
2	I think we should	____	**6**	In conclusion, I believe	____
3	In my view	____	**7**	a conclusion I would draw	____
4	a meaning that I share	____	**8**	if you ask me	____

---

benefit *Vorteil*

to shut the stable door after the horse has bolted *den Brunnen erst zudecken, wenn das Kind hineingefallen ist*

to exploit *sich etw zunutze machen*

to arouse *erwecken*

affirmation *Bestätigung*

to affect *beeinflussen*

face-to-face *persönlich*

physical exercise *Bewegung*

mental health *psychische Gesundheit*

curated *kuratiert*

vain *eingebildet*

to portray *abbilden*

artificial *künstlich*

to boast *prahlen*

to earn a living (from) *seinen Lebensunterhalt verdienen*

impressionable *beeinflussbar*

repetitive *wiederholend*

to subscribe *abonnieren*

to be a good/bad influence *von gutem/schlechtem Einfluss sein*

hit *Treffer*

to publish *veröffentlichen*

clickbait *Klickfang*

sensationalist *Sensations-*

legitimate *seriös*

to manipulate sb/sth *beeinflussen, manipulieren*

misinformation *Falschinformation*

echo chamber *Hallraum (der nur die eigene Meinung verstärkt)*

contentious *strittig*

offensive *beleidigend*

defamatory *diffamierend*

hate speech *Hassrede*

to get into trouble *Ärger bekommen*

to add fuel to the fire *Öl ins Feuer schütten*

to cotton on (to sth) *etw kapieren*

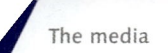

2 a You can find the highlighted words from the text on page 41 in the table below.
Fill in the empty boxes. In the 'Memory support' column box you can …
- put the word or phrase in a sentence, or
- think of words belonging to the same family, or, write down other collocations.

Word/Phrase	Memory support	German
to **exploit sb/sth**	Tabloid newspapers exploit our interest in the lives of the rich and famous.	
to **be addictive**	**WORD FAMILY** to be addicted to sth (vb) addiction (n) addict (n)	
	OTHER COLLOCATIONS to ~ curiosity / anger / fear / hatred	etw (z.B. Neugier, Zorn, Furcht, Hass etc.) erwecken / wecken
to **affect sb/sth**		jdn/etw betreffen, beeinflussen
to **portray**	The media often portray today's teens as slaves to their smartphones.	
	OTHER COLLOCATIONS to ~ a product banner / pop-up / hidden / commercial / paid / full-page / political / misleading ads (advertisements)	werben
brand	**OTHER COLLOCATIONS**	Handelsmarke
	WORD FAMILY to ~ to a newspaper / magazine / streaming provider subscription (n) subscriber (n)	abonnieren
to **publish**	The broadsheet newspapers didn't publish the photos of Prince Harry and Megan's children.	
sensationalist	Sensationalist journalism mostly consists of stories of scandal and divorces.	
to **manipulate sb/sth**		manipulieren
rumour		Gerücht
bias	**WORD FAMILY** to bias sb/sth bias (n) biased (in favour of / towards / against) (adj)	
	WORD FAMILY to report (on); reporter (n) reporting (n)	Bericht
	OTHER COLLOCATIONS to ~ a threat / a problem / a danger	etw darstellen

b Make eight words from 'Words in context'. Use each prefix or suffix once with the base words. Write the new words in the table.

Prefix	Base word	Suffix	New words	
	addict			
	agree			
dis-	content	-able		
mis-	impression	-ious		
mis-	information	-ive		
re-	post	-ize		
	leading			
	social			

c The collocations in the text below got mixed up. Write the highlighted words in their correct places so that the text makes sense.

growing

The ~~sensationalist~~ trend to spend more time online means that companies are using needs marketing increasingly often. Hit posts with growing headlines, content topics and controversial or familiar images have a much higher web rate than other forms of marketing. When it is done correctly, this kind of advertising can capture the emotional clickbait of the viewers and drive them towards inspiring and relevant contentious.

d Find English sayings in 'Words in context' which match the meanings below.

1 To make a conflict or a bad situation worse:

2 To try and stop something bad happening after it has already happened:

3 To begin to understand a situation or fact:

e Idioms and sayings can rarely be translated word for word. Try and find a German version of these sayings or write your own interpretation.

Children and fools speak the truth. – Proverb

A storm in a teacup. – Idiom

To pour oil on troubled waters. – Unknown

There are three kinds of lies: lies, damned lies, and statistics. – Benjamin Disraeli

A lie can be halfway around the world before the truth gets its boots on. – Mark Twain

Getting to grips with grammar

Do after Sections C and E

G ► Conditionals
SB, p.171

1 Conditional forms

> The choice between the **first conditional** and **second conditional** often depends on our point of view and how possible we feel a situation in the present or future is.
> To help remember how we form the first and second conditionals, think about the *if*-clause:
> **First conditional:** 'if' and 'will' makes me ill. **Second conditional:** 'if' and 'would' isn't good.
> The **third conditional** describes a past situation. Try to memorise an example: *If I had known it was your birthday, I would have baked you a cake.* (But I didn't know, and I didn't bake you a cake.)

Complete the sentences with the correct conditional forms: first, second or third.

1 If people _____ (**have to**) use their real names online, I think they _____ (**be**) nicer to each other on social media.

2 Don't deactivate your social media. How _____ I (**know**) what you are doing if you _____ (**do**) that? Don't expect me to actually visit you!

3 I _____ (**not have**) as many friends if social media _____ (**not exist**).

4 I read that Tim Berners-Lee invented the internet. But I think if he _____ (**not do**) it, someone else _____ (**invent**) it at some time.

5 I think Rob should take down that photo of Tim he posted. If Tim _____ (**see**) it, he_____ (**never talk**) to Rob again. It's so embarrassing.

6 If you _____ (**delete**) that strange message, the virus _____ (**not damage**) your PC.

G ► Used to SB,
p.173

2 Talking about the past with *used to*

> We use the **simple past** to talk about situations and actions which started and finished in the past, often with time phrases like: *ago, last Monday/week/month/..., yesterday.* If we want to describe habits or situations that happened regularly in the past, but do not now, we can use
> ***used to / didn't use to***.

Complete the sentences with ***used to*** where possible. If not, use the **simple past**.

My dad says things _____ (be) better before the internet. He _____ (visit)

his friends every day when he was a kid. Apparently, people _____ (not phone) each

other as often as we do now. In the old days, phone calls _____ (be) very expensive.

Dad's parents weren't so strict, but then one day the phone bill _____ (cost) so much

that Dad _____ (not get) any pocket money for two months! Dad thinks people

_____ (not feel) as stressed before the internet. They _____ (not have)

news apps with constant updates about all the problems in the world. And they _____

(not get) emails after work either. But older people *always* say the good old days _____

(be) better!

3 Describing activities in the past: past progressive

We use the **past progressive** to describe activities *around* a certain point of time in the past.
We form this tense with *was/were (not)* + *-ing* form of the verb.
At 4 pm yesterday, we **were playing** Fourth Knight in Brian's house.
It **wasn't raining** at lunchtime.

G ▸ *The past progressive SB, p. 164*

a A college teacher asks her students what they were doing at 11 o'clock last Saturday morning. Complete the sentences with the correct past progressive form of the verbs in the box.

do | help | lie | not do | ~~prepare~~ | shoot | shop | work | write

1 Orla: I *was preparing* the slides for my Economics presentation.

2 Salomé: I'm not sure. I think I _____ my dad in the garden.

3 Ben: I can't remember what I _____ at 11 am.

4 Richard: I was with my mum. We _____ for a new laptop.

5 Jenny: I had a late night on Friday so I _____ in bed at that time on Saturday.

6 Ben: I remember now! I _____ a long email to my cousin in America.

7 Brian: I think Abdullah and I _____ on our Economics homework, like Orla.

8 Abdullah: No, Brian, we _____ homework. We _____ a video!

Simple past or **past progressive**
We use the simple past to describe past actions that follow one another: *First, Marie **took** some photos in the park. Then she **posted** the best ones.*
We use the **past progressive** to give background information
*The sun **was shining** <u>when</u> Marie **took** the photos in the park.*
Decide which action or activity was short and which was long.
*I **saw** Marie in the park <u>while</u> I **was cycling** to town.*
*(I **saw** Marie – short action / I **was cycling** - longer activity)*
! State verbs do not have a progressive form, e.g. *know, have* (haben, besitzen), *like, love, hate,* etc.

b Use the verbs in brackets in the simple past or past progressive to complete the sentences.

1 I *was crossing* the road when the accident *happened*. (**cross, happen**)

2 Paul _____ to music so he _____ the phone. (**listen, not hear**)

3 My laptop _____ just as I _____ a video, so I lost the file. (**shut down, upload**)

4 I knew Nora was online because I _____ on my messaging app that she _____. (**see, text**)

5 Tabloid journalists _____ when the politician _____ at his home. (**wait, arrive**)

6 Keith _____ on the internet when he _____ his friend's secret blog. (**search, find**)

7 A thief _____ Julie's smartphone out of her hand while she _____ on it. (**grab, talk**)

8 I _____ the red light because I _____ at my phone. (**not notice, look**)

Stats & pics: Internet usage

Do after Section A

How young people aged 12–19 in Germany use the internet across all devices 2010–2020 – in per cent

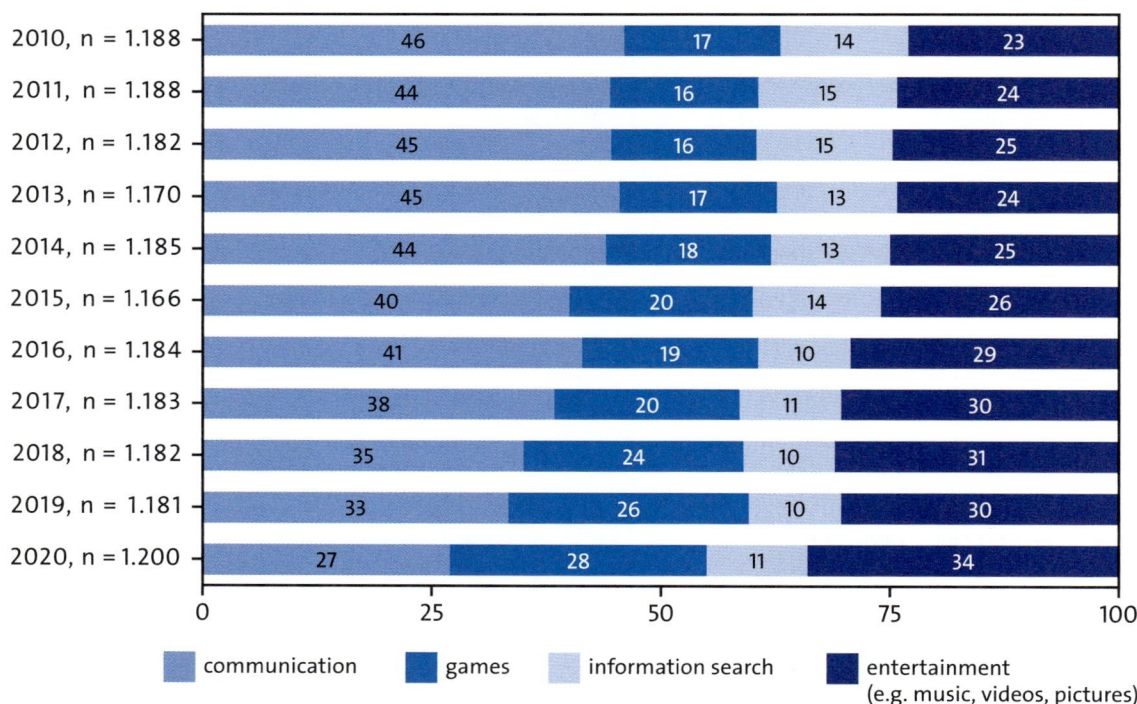

source: JIM 2010–JIM 2020, JIM survey 2020, figures for internet use given in percentages

1 Where is the chart taken from and when was it published?

_____

2 Complete the sentences about the chart with the verb forms below. There are three forms too many.

are using | falling | had fallen | has gradually gone down | has risen | reached | remained | rose | went down

1 Between 2010 and 2014, the figures showing how young people used the internet

_____ more or less the same.

2 Young people's use of the internet for research _____ a peak in 2011 and 2012 at 15%.

3 Since 2014, however, the amount of time spent using the internet for communication and research _____ .

4 For example, in 2014, young people spent 44% of their internet time communicating, but by 2020 the percentage _____ by 17% to 27%.

5 In contrast, the chart clearly shows young people _____ the internet more and more for games and entertainment, including streaming music and videos.

6 In 2010, nearly a quarter of their internet time was spent on entertainment but since then it ____ to just over a third.

How to say or write it

The chart is taken from …
It was published in …
The chart gives an overview of …
The chart is made up of …

There is a (clear/significant) trend to …
Between … and …, the amount of time spent … remained the same/dropped/rose.
Over the last … years, the amount of time people spend using the internet to … has increased/risen/decreased/gone down.

Writing workshop: Writing a summary

Do after Section D

1 Read this text about social media influencers. What type of text is it?

Look at page 76 in your student's book for help.

The rise of the 'genuinfluencers'

The influencer is dead. Long live the Genuinfluencers. By Priya Elan

"Genuinfluencers" was coined by the trend forecasters WGSN (formerly Worth Global Style Network) to describe social media stars who use their platforms beyond product placement. "The genuinfluencer does not specialise in fashion, beauty or lifestyle content," says WGSN's Cassandra Napoli. Instead, the creators "spread important information that can keep people informed", in addition to posts about products.

A recent Vogue Business article pointed to the likes of Munroe Bergdorf (the model and activist who discusses racial injustice and LGBTQ+ rights) and Frankie Bridge (the former Saturdays singer who speaks openly about her depression) as "genuinfluencers to watch". In the same year that the "fake news" era ended as Trump exited the White House and the Kardashian/Jenner clan axed their long-running show, Keeping Up With the Kardashians, the era of showboating excess and aspirational product placement has been eclipsed by something oppositional and grounded.

"Being too 'aspirational' is seen as almost repellent now by many generation-Zers, who favour platforms such as TikTok because of this," says trend forecaster Geraldine Wharry. [...] "Influencers are expected to be more authentic now, more than ever," says Wharry. "Transparency is also required. Influencers can easily come under fire if they use the wrong historical term or show any behaviour seen (at odds with the) highly informed gen-Zers."

The move towards greater transparency has been a long time coming. In 2017, the Federal Trade Commission published suggested guidelines as to how influencers should conduct themselves online, with a call for more clarity about their corporate relationships. [...] But it wasn't until the pandemic that this process sped up. At a time when people were stuck at home thinking about their mental health as well as the climate crisis and the Black Lives Matter movement, the role of the influencer had to morph.

"Instead of watching stories of celebrities who were saying: 'We're all in this together,' from their mansions, people wanted to (see) people going through the same difficult times," says Alessandro Bogliari, the co-founder of The Influencer Marketing Factory. "Because of the pandemic there has been a big shift from 'worshipping' celebs to trying to have a more 'normal' connection with influencers who were struggling as well."

Throughout 2020, influencers across the world expanded their roles, providing key information about the pandemic. "Influencers joined cultural conversations about important topics such as getting the vaccine and donating blood," Bogliari says. "Finland tapped 1,500 influencers to share (Covid) information with their networks and the UK government opted to pay a Love Island star to post NHS (National Health Service) information," says Napoli. "We saw sponsored TikTok dance routines encouraging audiences to wash their hands." She also points to TikTok creator Tinx (who Vogue called the platform's "big sister") and her video conversation with Dr Anthony Fauci, the US's top infectious diseases expert, about getting vaccinated. "In 2020, social media users logged on to learn. Social media platforms transitioned from spaces of inspiration to spaces of information and education."

A big change, too, he says, was that brands stopped looking at the number of followers an influencer has and instead at the influencer's audience. "Today, it is very hard for influencers and even brands not to disclose where they stand, for fear of being cancelled," says Wharry. "The audience wants to know so that they can make informed choices as to whom they follow or purchase from, as they see their follows, likes and cash as a way to show their political stance." Jeff Fromm, author of *Marketing To Gen Z*, says: "People in Gen Z are wise beyond their years and know how to turn their ideas into meaningful actions."

(611 words. Source: The Guardian, 12 August 2021)

2 Look at this checklist for writing a summary. Then read the example below and circle five of the rules a) – h) which it does not follow.

Checklist for summaries	
a Write your summary in the simple present.	**e** Your summary should follow the main arguments of the text in the same order.
b Name the title of the text, its author, source and year of publication.	**f** Use your own words. Do not include direct quotations from the article.
c Name the type of text: e.g. newspaper report, leading article, editorial, special feature, speech, comment, etc.	**g** Stay neutral and objective. Do not offer your own opinion.
d Structure your summary with: i) introduction, ii) main part, iii) conclusion.	**h** Your summary should be a quarter to a third of the length of the original text.

The text 'The rise of the genuinfluencers' written by Priya Elan and published in The Guardian in 2021 deals with the topic of social media influencers. In particular, the author claims that many influencers have become more serious and try to give their followers important information instead of only promoting products.

A big change mentioned in the article is that brands stopped thinking so much about how many   5
followers influencers have and more about the type of followers. The author quotes a trend forecaster who says that young people expect influencers to be more who they really are. Another
marketer says that during the pandemic, people did not want to see rich celebrities sending messages from their big houses, but rather people who were having problems just like they were. The
author believes that influencers had to stop only advertising products to keep their followers be-   10
cause "people were stuck at home thinking about their mental health as well as the climate crisis
and the Black Lives Matter movement". The author shares information from other people who say
that in 2020 influencers worked with governments in Finland and the UK to provide information
on Covid and that in the same year people who use social media used it more to learn and educate
themselves. I think this point is true, but it is only a small number of influencers. So I do not   15
agree with the author's view that 'influencers are dead'.

In her concluding paragraph the author quotes an expert in marketing who says that people are
using their likes and money as a way of showing support for influencers who agree with their
politics. As a result, the expert says, influencers are afraid of being cancelled. This expert also says
that Gen-Z young people are intelligent and can turn their ideas into positive actions.   20

(301 words)

3 a Go back to the original article and ==highlight== the most important information in it.

b Note down the main arguments from the text in a table like the one below.

Then use your notes and the checklist in 2 to do exercise 4.

Lines	Arguments
1–2	'Genuinfluencers' is a new term, they post about more than just products

4 Read the text 'The rise of the genuinfluencers' and outline how Generation Z expects influencers to change and the effects this has had on the behaviour of social media stars.

Mediation: A question of trust

Do after Section B

1 Read the text below and do the tasks which follow it.

Maria Bergmann ist eine vierzigjährige, gut ausgebildete Wissenschaftlerin, die für ein großes Pharmaunternehmen arbeitet. Aufgewachsen in Greifswald, Mecklenburg-Vorpommern, war sie es gewohnt, dass immer Zeitungen auf dem Küchentisch und im Wohnzimmer lagen. Sie selbst hatte bis vor etwa fünf Jahren sowohl ein Magazin für aktuelle Themen als auch eine Ta-
5 geszeitung abonniert. Sie hat beide gekündigt. Zwar hat sich die Auflage der gedruckten Zeitungen in Frau Bergmanns Lebenszeit halbiert, aber der Trend zur Digitalisierung der Nachrichten ist nicht der Grund, warum sie ihre Print-Abonnements gekündigt hat. Warum dann?

„Ich bin ein logischer, rationaler und intelligenter Mensch. Ich will mir nicht vorschreiben lassen, wie ich zu denken habe", sagt sie. Frau Bergmann ist der Meinung, dass die Journalisten der
10 traditionellen Presse nicht mehr neutral sind. „Bestimmte Themen werden nicht mehr debattiert. Es scheint Überzeugungen zu geben, die die meisten Journalisten haben, und auch wenn sie es nicht direkt sagen, muss der Leser diese akzeptieren, weil wir so denken sollen."

Frau Bergmann scheint Teil eines wachsenden Trends zu sein. Jüngste Umfragen zeigen, dass vier von zehn Deutschen der Meinung sind, dass die Medien in gewissem Maße die Wahrheit
15 verzerren und Fakten verbergen, und dass sie ihnen deshalb nicht voll vertrauen. Fast jeder Fünfte sagt, dass er den großen Medienunternehmen überhaupt nicht vertraut.

Und woher bezieht Frau Bergmann nun ihre Nachrichten? „Ich schaue immer noch manchmal die Abendnachrichten im Fernsehen, und ich lese die traditionellen Nachrichtenmedien im Internet. Aber ich bin offen für andere Quellen: „Search", soziale Netzwerke und soziale Medien."
20 Sie gibt zu, dass sie Blogs und Websites von Kommentatoren liest, die manche für extrem halten.

„Ich habe nicht das Gefühl, dass ich von den großen Medienorganisationen ein vollständiges Bild erhalte. Deshalb besuche ich manchmal Websites, die ganz offen ihre Agenda und ihre Voreingenommenheit offenlegen – egal ob sie rechts oder links sind. Als Wissenschaftler bin ich sehr vorsichtig mit dem, was man mir als „Fakten" vorsetzt, und ich weiß, dass es viele Fehlinfor-
25 mationen gibt. Ich vertraue nur dem, was sich belegen lässt – alles andere ist Meinung. Aber ich möchte alle Meinungen hören, damit ich selbst entscheiden kann, was ich denke."

(348 words)

2 How are the following terms expressed in German in the text?

circulation (l. 5)	recent (l. 13)	sources (l. 19)
subscriptions (l. 7)	to a certain extent (l. 14)	bias (l. 23)
beliefs (l. 9)	distort (l. 15)	back up (l. 25)

3 Answer the questions on the text in English.

1 What has happened to the sales of printed news publications in the last four decades?

2 What does Ms Bergmann think about the traditional news media?

3 Why do some Germans say they do not fully trust the media in their country?

4 How does Ms Bergmann deal with the risk of misinformation?

Going deeper

You are going to listen to a discussion about correcting misinformation.

Before you listen

How would you deal with misinformation which a family member or a friend shared with you online?

- [ ] Report the person to the social network
- [ ] Tell them they are wrong
- [ ] Ignore the misinformation or the person
- [ ] Share the correct information with them
- [ ] Threaten to block the person if they share it again
- [ ] Thank the person and ask for more information

🔊 While listening
05

1 Tick the correct answer (a, b, or c). There is only one correct answer.

1 Miriam talks about an example of misinformation which
- **a** ... she shared by accident.
- **b** ... doesn't really exist.
- **c** ... her auntie posted online.

2 Miriam says that when someone shares misinformation with you, you should
- **a** ... react quickly to stop the person embarrassing themselves.
- **b** ... just send them a link to an article with the correct information.
- **c** ... react in a positive way at first.

2 Match the effects A–E to the actions below. There is one more effect than you need.

A Increases the chance the other person will accept accurate information   **B** gives the other person a chance to correct themselves   **C** shows the other person a good example

D creates common ground between you   **E** can help the person to reflect on what they believe

Showing that you are open-minded   **Asking questions**

_____   _____

3 Listen again and complete the sentences.

1 It is easier to accept that we are wrong when we _____.

2 You should _____ when you explain why the misinformation is wrong.

3 Be careful not to include _____ in your correction.

4 You should not be afraid to _____ if you see that somebody has already corrected your friend's/relative's misinformation.

5 Correcting misinformation should be seen as a way _____ each other.

Fun & games

Do after Topic 4

1 Who said it?

These quotations were said by the eight activists from section C of your student's book. But who said what? Use the internet to find out and write the name of the activist beside the quotation.

"I've probably earned the right to screw up a few times. I don't want the fear of failure to stop me from doing what I really care about."	_____
"Change happens by listening and then starting a dialogue with the people who are doing something you don't believe is right."	_____
"Do not judge me by my successes, judge me by how many times I fell down and got back up again."	_____
"Unless you have dialogue, unless you open the walls of dialogue, you can never reach to change people's opinion."	_____
"... we have to tell it like it is. Because if there are no positive things to tell, then what should we do, should we spread false hope? We can't do that, we have to tell the truth."	_____
"When the whole world is silent, even one voice becomes powerful."	_____
"If I cannot do great things, I can do small things in a great way."	_____
"You must be the change you wish to see in the world."	_____

2 How social media began

Match the social media apps with the correct description. Then match the year it first appeared.

Facebook Snapchat TikTok Twitter Whatsapp YouTube	2003 2005 2007 2009 2011 2014	
	Social media	Launched
The first version of this was meant to be a way of creating and sharing short educational videos between three and five minutes long.	_____	_____
It began first as a kind of SMS app that let you send short messages to a small group of people.	_____	_____
The very first version was for university students to say how attractive other students were.	_____	_____
This app began as a simple app which let you simply write what you were doing at the time, e.g. I just woke up.	_____	_____
This began as a way to share videos and clips. The first video on the site was a 19-second clip of one of the founders visiting the zoo.	_____	_____
First called Picaboo, three university students came up with the idea of this social media app where photos and videos would disappear shortly after being posted.	_____	_____

3 DYKYA? → Do you know your abbreviations?

Write out the 12 abbreviations from texting and social media in full.

TIP: Those in black are from Topic 4. If you do not know those in blue – look them up on the internet!

OMGIDKLMKROFLBTWTTYLTBHBRBIMOLOLTGIFIRL

1 _____ 7 _____

2 _____ 8 _____

3 _____ 9 _____

4 _____ 10 _____

5 _____ 11 _____

6 _____ 12 _____

4 Word search: Media, old and new

Find 14 words in the word search. Seven refer to more modern media and seven to traditional forms.

The words are across → or down ↓.

New media

A __ __ __ __ __ __ __ __

__ __ __ __ chamber

E __ __ __ __

F __ __ __ __ __ __ __

S __ __ __ __ __ __ __ __

__ __ __ __ __ __ advertising

__ __ __ __ message

Traditional media

M __ __ __ __ __ __ __

N __ __ __ __ __ __ __ __

public service __ __ __ __ __ __ __ __ __ __ __

quality __ __ __ __ __

radio __ __ __ __ __ __ __

T __ __ __ __ __ __

TV __ __ __ __ __ __ __

F	O	L	L	O	W	E	R	S	M	F	D	P	F
Y	P	J	C	A	J	E	U	L	O	B	X	R	M
X	D	H	H	M	M	A	G	A	Z	I	N	E	G
T	E	X	T	I	L	C	Q	C	X	B	Q	S	K
A	V	C	T	B	E	P	D	K	G	P	V	S	J
B	R	O	A	D	C	A	S	T	E	R	G	O	B
L	O	S	L	I	H	T	T	I	T	O	V	P	C
O	B	P	G	S	O	G	G	V	V	G	Q	C	T
I	H	R	O	H	K	P	M	I	C	R	B	N	A
D	K	T	R	G	N	E	W	S	P	A	P	E	R
C	S	B	I	R	K	R	O	T	C	M	I	W	G
S	T	A	T	I	O	N	D	F	A	M	H	U	E
L	B	T	H	J	H	O	T	C	O	E	H	Q	T
Y	F	E	M	O	J	I	S	G	S	G	J	B	E
J	A	H	O	B	V	N	G	N	S	J	N	C	D

Writing a comment

1 You are going to write a comment in which you give your personal opinion on a statement. Before that, complete tasks a) – d) which will help you examine the structure of a comment and phrases you can use.

a Here is a sample comment on the statement: "Gen-Z is Gen 'Me': the most selfish generation yet".

Read it. Then do task b).

Introduction	1 The statement talks about Gen-Z, meaning the generation born after 1995, as a selfish generation because it says young people think about 'me', that is themselves. 2 I disagree. 3 In this comment, I will first look at arguments behind why someone might make such a statement and then I will put forward my own view that I, along with most of my peers, are in fact maybe the opposite: the most selfless generation yet.
Main body (1)	4 Firstly, for older people, who didn't grow up with smartphones, the fact that young people take a lot of selfies is used as an argument that members of Gen-Z place too much importance on how they look. 5 In addition, the trend of young people sharing their lives on social media can give the impression that Gen-Zers only think about themselves. When older people see young people in groups all staring at their phones, 6 for instance, it understandably leads to the conclusion that they are all busy in their own individual 'bubbles'. 7 However, it is too simple to make such judgements based on what it seems young people are doing. Let's look at the other side.
Main body (2)	8 While it is true to say young people take a lot of selfies, they do not put more importance on how they look than previous generations. After all, make up and personal care products have existed for a long time. 9 Whereas young people today post their lives online, past generations kept diaries or wrote to friends by letter. 10 Furthermore, it is not true to say young people are not 'together' when they use their smartphones. Very often, they are playing online games together or 'chatting' with each other. It is only the technology that has changed, not people themselves. 11 Lastly and most importantly, we should ask ourselves what young people really are doing today? Young people are organising themselves to hold climate strikes and to march against gun violence, 12 to give two examples. Thanks to social media, Gen-Z knows what problems people have all around the world in real-time and they care. Young people are more involved in finding solutions to these problems through online and offline activism. Greta Thunberg and Malala Yousafzai are excellent examples of Gen-Z.
Conclusion	13 To sum up, while it is understandable that some older people think Gen-Z is all about 'me', it is a mistake. 14 In my opinion, Gen-Z knows more about the problems other people face and cares more about finding solutions than previous generations. 15 For this reason, I come to the conclusion that the original statement should be rewritten as: Gen-Z is Gen 'Us': the most caring generation yet.

Line numbers: 5, 10, 15, 20, 25, 30

b Look at the underlined phrases in the comment above. Think about their purpose. Now match the phrase numbers with the purposes below. The first is done for you.

Balancing an argument with a counter argument: 7 , _____ , _____

Defining the topic: _____

Drawing a conclusion: _____ , _____

Expressing a personal opinion: _____ , _____

Giving arguments a logical order: _____ , _____ , _____ , _____

Giving examples: _____ , _____

Outlining what the writer is going to do: _____

c You are going to comment on the statement 'The generation gap has never been wider'. As preparation, look at some ideas below and brainstorm some more points. You should decide first whether you are going to agree or disagree with the statement. Then write your rough ideas in the table in d).

In agreement with the statement	*In disagreement with the statement*
young people are much more tolerant and open to diversity than older people ...	*the generation gap is not a new concept: it is a normal part of adolescence for young people to disagree with older people*
Older people cannot understand the digital world young people live in ...	*Older people aren't as conservative as some say: without older people we wouldn't have same-sex marriage today*

d Use the table to plan the structure of your comment.

Introduction	Main body (1)	Main body (2)	Conclusion
Define the topic.			Finish with your opinion.

e Now complete the exam task: **Comment on the statement 'The generation gap has never been wider'.**

Remember to use phrases from a) and b) in your answer.
Write on a separate sheet of paper, if you need more space.
Look back at pages 35–40 in your student's book for more help.

Introduction	
Main body (1)	
Main body (2)	
Conclusion	

Doing a creative writing task

1 You are going to do the following task:

Read the following newspaper editorial about the English education system. Write a letter for publication to the editor in which you give your own view. Support your view with your own personal experience as a student in Germany.

Look at p. 41 in your student's book if you need help.

Before you do the task, complete exercises a) – d).

a Read the editorial article below and highlight the key information it contains on i) end-of-year exams and ii) continuous assessment. Use two different colours.

The Covid-19 pandemic created chaos and stress for students studying for their A-Level exams in 2020. It showed how using end-of-year exams may not be the best way of evaluating students' academic performance. Now, some experts want the exams to be cancelled in favour of continuous assessment. Supporters of the current A-Levels say they are an effective way of
5   measuring the ability of students to demonstrate what they have learnt in a pressurised situation – a real life skill, they say. But critics say that end-of-year exams only measure someone's ability to *do exams*. They say it is only a snapshot of a person's ability on one particular day and does not show how hard a student has worked over the course of their studies. It rewards last-minute, intensive study just before an exam, and measures only students' memory, not intelli-
10   gence. Supporters of continuous assessment say multiple examples of students' work over two years, such as project work and shorter written tests, can be used to create a grade point average, similar to the system used in the United States. This, they claim, would spread the stress over a longer time and would reward students' efforts during the whole of their final two years of second-level education. Critics of continuous assessment say that this would not be objective
15   because students are graded by their own teachers. They believe that without a final standardised test, the education system would lose a key measure of how well it serves students. Some teachers also point out the increased workload on teachers of a continuous assessment system. Some feel that teachers will suffer stress when they are responsible for deciding their students' futures. Another risk is that students could feel under pressure to achieve good grades for the
20   whole two years. This newspaper feels the answer, as usual, lies somewhere in the middle: a mixed system which gives sixty percent of a student's final grade to in-school work over two years and the remaining forty per cent to final exams.

b Before you brainstorm ideas for your text, answer the questions in the table below.

What type of text do I have to produce? (speech, article, letter, etc.)	Who am I writing/ speaking to? (an audience, school magazine readers, newspaper editor, newspaper readers etc.)	What kind of language should I use? (formal, informal)	What is the purpose of my text? (to convince, to give my opinion, to share facts, etc.)

c Brainstorm ideas for your text on a sheet of paper. One of the graphic organisers on p.42 of your student's book can help you. You will need to decide what your opinion/response is going to be. TIP: It does not have to be your real opinion/response, but it should be one you think you can write best about.

d Before you write your text, create a rough outline of your text in the table below. Use the information you highlighted in a) and your ideas from c).

Introduction / Opening

Main body of your text

Conclusion/closing

2 Now complete the writing task on a separate sheet of paper:

Read the following newspaper editorial about the English education system. Write a letter for publication to the editor in which you give your own view. Support your view with your own personal experience as a student in Germany.

Analysing and describing charts and graphs

a Before you describe the graph, do this grammar check. Translate the German sentences below into English.

Look at pp. 70–71 in your student's book for help.

1 In einigen Jahren werden sich die Zahlen auf den Wert von 20.. erholt haben.

In a few years, the figures will have recovered to their value of 20.. .

2 Vom 20.. bis 20.. blieb der Prozentsatz relativ stabil.

_____

3 In den letzten # Jahren sind die Zahlen stetig gestiegen.

_____

4 Der aktuelle Trend zeigt, dass der Wert von XYZ steigt.

_____

5 Im Jahr 20.. stürzte der Wert von XYZ auf einen Tiefstand von #.

_____

6 Der Prozentsatz hat seinen früheren Höchststand noch nicht wieder erreicht.

_____

b Describe the graph of New Zealand's tourism sector's past and forecasted future share of Gross Domestic Product (GDP). Refer to the impact of the Covid-19 pandemic.

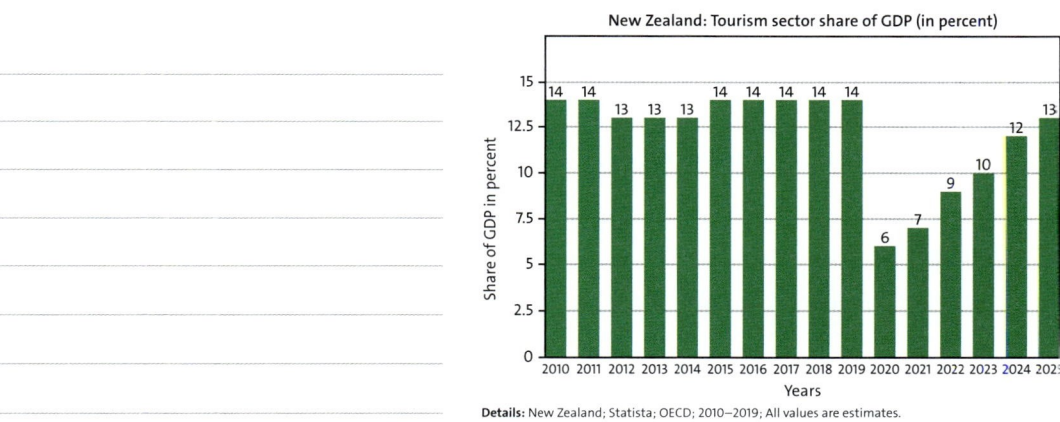

New Zealand: Tourism sector share of GDP (in percent)

Details: New Zealand; Statista; OECD; 2010–2019; All values are estimates.

Presenting

Look at pp. 74–75 in your student's book for help.

a It can be helpful, when giving a presentation, to imagine that you are taking your audience on a tour of your home. Look at the image below. The presentation/tour begins at your front door and each room is a stage in your talk.

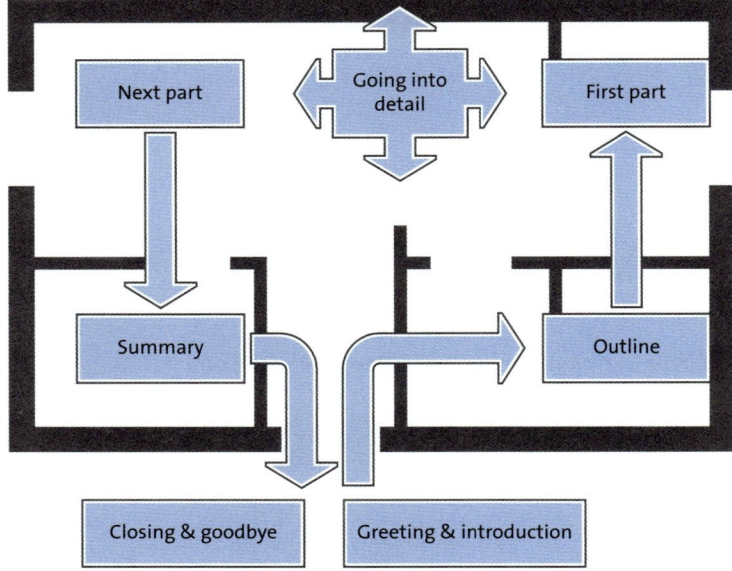

b Complete the underlined gaps in the phrases used to signpost the different parts of your presentation. Use the verbs from the box. The first one has been done for you.

discuss • expand • finish • give • giving • giving • interrupt • look make • moving • remember • remind • saying • summarize • ~~talk~~ • turn

Introducing yourself and your topic

Today I am going to ___talk___ to you about ...   I'll start off by _____ you a brief overview.

There are a number of points I'd like to _____ . First of all, ... , Then I'll talk about ... .

I'll _____ with ... .

If you have any questions → please don't hesitate to _____ me. / I'll gladly deal with them at the end.

Beginning new parts and moving between parts

Let's _____ first to ...   And now, _____ on to ...

Now, I'd like to _____ ...
The next topic I'd like to focus on is ...

Going into detail on a point

Let's _____ at that in more detail ...   I'd like to _____ on that if I may ...

Let me explain by _____ you an example ...

Ending your presentation

Let's _____ briefly what we've looked at.   Let me _____ you of some of the issues we've covered.

I would like to finish by _____ ...

c Choose one of the following topics and prepare a three-minute presentation. Write brief points, not a script, on flash cards. Practise by walking around your home as you talk. When you are ready, give your presentation and record yourself. If possible, ask somebody to listen to it and give you feedback.

- Why Banksy should/shouldn't be arrested. (Do an internet search if you do not know who Banksy is)
- Gentrification is destroying/is improving my town.
- What is great about living in my town.
- How we can encourage more people to use public transport.

Dealing with listening tasks

1 You are going to listen to a podcast with American students discussing American politics. Before you listen, do exercises 1 a) – e). This will help you practise how to analyse a listening task.

Look at pp. 104–105 in your student's book for help.

a Look at exercise 2 a). With listening exercises, it is very important to read the task carefully. Quickly note the key vocabulary from questions 1 and 2 below. Doing this will help you to predict what you will need to listen for.

1 Key vocabulary
reasons – to trust – politics

2 Key vocabulary
government – build more trust

b The audio material may include the same vocabulary from the task, but it often contains synonyms for the words in the task itself. Quickly note any synonyms or alternatives you can think of for the words you wrote in a). Write them beside or under the words in a).

c Now look at exercise 2 b). Read the sentence parts carefully. Make a note of any language features you notice. It can help you do the task if you have an idea of what type of grammar or collocations you can expect to hear.

Sentence 1	*will clause should come before an if + present simple clause /maybe people will vote more or trust more?*
Sentence 2	
Sentence 3	

d Now look at exercise 2 c). Read the possible answers carefully. Quickly brainstorm what you know about the items mentioned in each possible answer. Note your ideas in the box below.

US elections

e Now that you have completed exercises 1 a) – d), go on and do the listening exercises in 2.

You are going to listen to a student podcast where the host talks to two students, Jamal and Lindsey, about the issue of trust in politics.

a While you listen, choose the correct answers. There may be more than one correct answer.

1 What reasons do Jamal and Lindsey give for not having trust in politics at a local and federal level in the US?

    a ☐ Politicians only sign laws into force which companies like.
    b ☐ They feel they have no influence over local politics.
    c ☐ Corruption and dishonesty.
    d ☐ They have no personal connection with politicians at the national, federal level.

2 What do they think the government can do to build more trust with people?

    a ☐ Include people affected by government policy in government decision making.
    b ☐ Have more press conferences so journalists can ask the government questions.
    c ☐ Allow normal citizens to ask the government questions on live television.
    d ☐ Create a special ministry to deal with choices affecting minorities such as people of colour.

b Complete the sentences.

Jamal believes people _____ if they know that those with power share the same goals and interests as they do.

Lindsey thinks that these days you have to _____ if you want to be elected.

Jamal wonders when politicians get the time _____ the country and the planet are facing.

c The podcast host asks Jamal and Lindsey what they would change in the US political system if they had magic powers. Match three ideas to each speaker. There are two you do not need.

A Have more poor and ethnic minority candidates standing for election.

B Keep the Senate election process as it is.

C Stop millionaires from standing for election.

D Give public money to election candidates.

E Have elections for the House of Representatives at the same time as the presidential election.

F Limit the amount of money candidates can spend on election campaigns.

G Give Republicans and Democrats more time to work together.

H Reduce the number of members of the House of Representatives.

Lindsey: Jamal:

_____   _____

_____   _____

_____   _____

Using dictionaries

1 a Look at the monolingual (*einsprachig*) dictionary entry for the word *franchise*. Think about the theme of Topic 3.

Look at pp. 106–107 in your student's book for help.

| fran•chise¹ | /ˈfræntʃaɪz/ ☐ | ●○○ 7 | noun ☐ |

1a) [countable, uncountable] ☐ permission given by a company to someone who wants to sell its goods or services ☐

b) [countable] ☐ a business, shop etc that is run under franchise ☐

2 [countable] American English ☐ a professional sports team ☐

3 [uncountable] ☐ *formal* ☐ the legal right to vote in your country's elections ☐

b Where can you find the information 1–7? Write the numbers in the correct boxes above. One piece of information has been included as an example.
1 The meaning of the word most relevant to the theme of Topic 3 (one of the 4 green boxes)
2 The type of word
3 How the word is pronounced
4 If both singular and plural meanings of the word are possible
5 The style of the word
6 A geographical region where another meaning of the word exists
7 How often the word is used in English

2 a Use a monolingual dictionary to check the meanings of the words in the list below. Then write the words in the correct places in the text (1-5). You will need the definitions of the words for b).

clerk | motions | quorum | tally | tie

The Senate votes on bills, resolutions, **1** *motions*, amendments, nominations, and treaties in a variety of ways. If one-fifth of a **2** _____ of senators request it, the Senate will take a roll-call vote. In a roll-call vote, each senator votes "yea" or "nay" as his or her name is called by the **3** _____, who records the votes on a **4** _____ sheet. In most cases a simple majority is required for a measure to pass. In the case of a **5** _____, the vice president may cast the tie-breaking vote.

b Write in the definitions of the words which helped you decide the correct places in a)

1 *motion: a proposal that is made formally at a meeting, and then is usually decided on by voting*

2 _____

3 _____

4 _____

5 _____

c Now use a **bilingual** dictionary to find the best English word to fill the gaps in the text.

In a few instances, the Constitution requires a two-thirds vote of the Senate, including: expelling a senator; overriding a presidential veto; adopting a proposed constitutional 6 Gesetzesänderung *amendment*; convicting an 7 angeklagt _____ official; and consenting to ratification of a treaty. [...] Finally, much of Senate business is conducted by 8 einstimmig _____ consent, in which a 9 Maßnahme _____ passes so long as no senator 10 einwendet _____.

d The English words you chose may or may not be the same as the words used in the original text. That is acceptable if the word is a synonym and fits the context and style (formal/informal). You can compare your answers to the original in the 'About Voting' section of this page: **www. cop.senate.gov/about/powers-procedures/voting.htm**

Look at p. 108 in your student's book for help.

Stylistic devices

When analysing a text, it is not enough to know what stylistic devices a speaker/writer uses, but also *why* they are used and what effect these devices can have on the audience: listeners or readers. The lines which are quoted below are all taken from President Biden's July 2021 speech on voting (see p.34).

alliteration
Alliteration, Stabreim

citadel
Zitadelle, Festung

irony
Ironie

metaphor
Metapher

parallelism
Parallelismus

repetition
Wiederholung

rhetorical question
rhetorische Frage

a Use the words and phrases from the box below to complete the analysis of the stylistic devices Biden uses in his speech. There are some phrases you do not need.

• employs humour to make the point • Informal register/tone • Irony • makes the message more convincing • makes the situation easier to picture • Parallelism • Personification • repetition of the same sounds • Rhetorical question

"Well, folks, good afternoon."

Stylistic device: _____

Effect: A relaxed and familiar style makes the listeners feel as if they are on the same personal level as the speaker. The use of everyday spoken language such as 'folks' makes the speech seem more like a conversation with the audience so that they will be more open to listening to him.

"This is a test of our time and what I'm here to talk about today."

Stylistic device: Alliteration
Effect: The _____ and the rhythm makes it more memorable for the audience.

"A 102-year-old woman in Arkansas who voted for the first time ... A 94-year-old woman in Michigan ... All told, more than 150 million Americans [...] exercised their right to vote.

Stylistic device: Factual data
Effect: The speaker illustrates his point with concrete examples and statistical information.
This _____ , so listeners are more likely to believe what he is saying

"... the example of America at its best. But instead, we continue to see an example of human nature at its worst"

Stylistic device: _____
Effect: Repeating a structure emphasizes the speaker's message, while contrasting a positive phrase with a negative phrase makes a stronger impression on the audience.

"the Capitol, the citadel of our democracy"

Stylistic device: Metaphor
Effect: The speaker employs imagery which _____ for the audience. It also makes the message stronger and more memorable.

"America and Americans of every background voted. [...] In 2020, democracy was put to a test"

Stylistic device: _____
Effect: By talking about an object or thing as if it is a person, it is easier for the listeners to identify with them and feel an emotional reaction.

b Over to you: look at the stylistic device below. Find an example of it from Biden's speech (a different example than that used in the exercise on page 34) and write a statement about the effect it can have.

Example: _____

_____

Stylistic device: Repetition
Effect: _____

_____

_____

_____

_____

_____

_____

Describing and analysing cartoons and pictures

THE TRUTH

IGNORE THAT – SOCIAL MEDIA TELLS ME THAT THE TRUTH IS A CONSPIRACY TO KEEP US IN OUR PLACE.

CHRIS MADDEN

Look at pp. 136–137 in your student's book for help.

1 Describe and analyse the cartoon on the left by completing the sentences.

a General information

The cartoon was drawn by _____.

The cartoon deals with _____

_____

_____

b Description

In the foreground you can see _____

_____.

In the background in the top left corner, there is _____

_____ which _____

_____

_____ The man in the centre seems to be _____. The man in front is

_____

_____. A caption

on the right shows us that _____

_____

_____. The man behind is _____ and he seems to

_____.

c Interpret the cartoon

The point of the cartoon seems to be that _____

_____

The caption is ironic in the sense that _____

_____

_____.

Furthermore, there is some humour in the fact that _____.

_____

_____.

The man following behind might actually be _____

_____.

d Give your opinion on the effectiveness of the cartoon

In my opinion, the cartoonist makes his point / doesn't make his point effectively because _____

_____

_____

_____.

2 Look at the illustration and think about the theme and any message the picture might be trying to express.

a Note down your ideas.

_____

_____

_____

_____

_____

_____

_____

b Describe the picture.

_____

_____

_____

_____

_____

_____

Look at pp. 136–137 in your student's book for help.

_____

_____

_____

_____

_____

_____

_____

_____

_____

_____

How to say or write it

The picture is divided into …
… at the top/bottom (of the image) …
… on the left/right (of the image) …
… in the top-left/-right corner …
… in the bottom-left/right corner …
… in the foreground/background …
… in the centre (of the picture) …
The right-hand/left-hand part of the picture/image …
There is a prominent image of …
… shows a figure/person, seen from the back/side/front …
It/The picture features/depicts …
All around / Surrounding the (central) image, there are …
… in/with the shape of (a person/…)
These include …
It looks like (a man/he is doing sth) … …
He/She/It appears/seems (to be verb-ing) …
The person is wearing/doing/moving …

c Interpret the picture by completing the following texts in your own words.

What is the atmosphere expressed in each side of the image?

_____

_____

_____

_____

_____

How to say or write it

The atmosphere (of the picture) is negative/
dark/gloomy/hectic/calm/peaceful/
positive …
The image of (the person) conveys freedom/
lack of freedom/ a feeling of …
The red/blue/etc. colour suggests …
… contrasts (strongly) with … / forms a stark
contrast with …
Its atmosphere/The effect is achieved by …
The symbol(s) represent / stand for …

How is the atmosphere achieved?

The left-hand side: _____

_____

_____

_____

The right-hand side: _____

_____

_____

_____

d Evaluate the picture.

_____

_____

_____

_____

_____

_____

_____

_____

_____

How to say or write it

The image/photo/poster clearly illustrates/
doesn't clearly illustrate the idea/concept
of …
The artist's /illustrator's/photographer's
use of … / depiction of … succeeds/
doesn't succeed in expressing/effectively
expresses …
The message/point of the image is
(clearly)/seems to be …
The image/illustration (probably)
represents the opinion of someone who…
While it is …. , there is also …
Although the person/the image/…, the
other person/text/…
I think the artist is (partly) right,
because …
I (don't) agree / feel / find …
In my opinion/view, …

Analysing a text

1 You are going to analyse the text below. Before you do, read the text and complete tasks a) – f) which will help you prepare your analysis. As you read, it may help to use the traffic light reading strategy (see p.72 of your student's book).

I call on the world's tech giants, please don't put profit before safety

By Priti Patel, UK Home Secretary

Modern technology has brought many benefits, but any powerful medium also brings dangers. The internet and social media are used to conduct and facilitate the most despicable crimes.

[...] It is devastating for those it hurts and happens on a vast and growing scale. Last year, global
5   technology companies identified and reported 21 million instances of child sexual abuse.

[A] misconception is that this all takes place in dark corners of the web. In fact, much of this abuse occurs on everyday apps and platforms that you probably use for perfectly normal reasons.

End-to-end encrypted messaging presents a big challenge to public safety, and this is not just a matter for governments and law enforcement. Social media companies need to understand they
10 share responsibility for keeping people safe. [...]

Your messages are already encrypted as they travel from your device to a technology company's systems. End-to-end encryption takes this further, so that neither the platform operator nor police can see the content – even when it's essential for safety reasons that they do so.

[...] The introduction of end-to-end encryption must not open the door to even greater levels of
15 child sexual abuse – but that is the reality if plans such as those put forward by Facebook go ahead unchanged. Hyperbolic accusations from some quarters that this is really about governments wanting to snoop and spy on innocent citizens are simply untrue.

It is about keeping the most vulnerable among us safe and preventing truly evil crimes.

I am calling on our international partners and allies to continue to back the UK's approach of
20 holding technology companies to account and asking social media companies to put public safety before profits. They must not let harmful content continue to be posted on their platforms or neglect public safety when designing their products.

[...] Big Tech firms collectively need to take responsibility for public safety and greater investment is essential. Today, I am launching a new Safety Tech Challenge Fund. We will award five organi-
25 sations from around the world up to £85,000 each to develop innovative technology to keep children safe in environments such as online messaging platforms with end-to-end encryption. [...]

Modern technology has changed the world, in many ways for the better. We cannot allow it to be used to hurt children.
(394 words)   Abridged from: The Telegraph 8 September 2021

Home Secretary
Innenminister(in)
despicable
abscheulich
**end-to-end
encryption**
*Ende-zu-Ende-Ver-
schlüsselung*
hyperbolic
überzogen
accusation
Vorwurf
vulnerable
verwundbar

a Name the author of the text and say where and when it was published.

Look at p.140
in your
student's book
if you need
help.

b Look at page 138 of your student's book and decide what type of non-literary text you are dealing with.
Circle the correct alternatives in the sentence below.

The text is *a comment* / *an editorial* because it is mostly *informative* / *argumentative* and contains *clear conclusions and demands* / *a focus on objective facts*.

c Rewrite the sentence below to make it true for this text. Replace the underlined words with words from the text with the same meaning. The line numbers are given to help you.

The author employs a neutral register. This is indicated by simple sentence structures and vocabulary such as <u>carry out</u> (l.3), <u>terrible</u> (l.3) and <u>misunderstanding</u> (l.6).

_____

_____

d While a text can have an overall tone, it may change in tone e.g. begin in a light-hearted way and then become more serious. Choose four adjectives from the list to complete the description of this article's tone.

aggressive   determined   dramatic   humorous   ironic
light-hearted   sarcastic   serious   warning   witty

The author sets a very _____ tone at the beginning of the text and by using words such as "dangers", "despicable crimes" and "devastating" she creates a _____ atmosphere. As the text goes on, the tone changes into a _____ tone especially in line XX "but that is the reality if ...". Towards the end of the text, the tone becomes strong and _____ as indicated by "They must not let" and "We cannot allow" as the author ends her text with a firm call to action.

e Focus on the main parts of the text. It helps to make short notes or one-line summaries of the points the author makes. Write two points from the list below into each section on the next page where they are mentioned in the article above. Two of the points are not needed.

- A lot of child abuse happens on the internet.
- End-to-end encryption should not be allowed.
- Facebook should change its plan for end-to-end encryption.
- Governments need to spy on citizens for their own safety.
- Increasing the privacy of social media apps could put children at greater risk.
- Keeping the internet safe is not only a matter for governments and the police.
- More money needs to be spent by internet companies to protect people.
- The UK wants to encourage firms to invent new ways of protecting young internet users.

1. Introduction and first part (ll. 1–10)	
2. Second part (ll. 11–22)	
3. Final part and conclusion (ll. 23–28)	

f Analysing a text often means saying what stylistic devices are used by an author and what effect they have. Complete the sentences below with the correct stylistic device. There is one you do not need.

alliteration | directly addressing | factual data | metaphors | posing a rhetorical question | repetition

1 Following the introduction, the author supports her arguments with _____

– "21 million instances" – this shocking information should persuade readers that her points are

important and should be supported.

2 The author refers to her readers when she says, "platforms that you probably use", "your

messages" and "your device". By _____ the readers, she attracts their

attention to the fact that this issue affects them personally and she hopes to convince them to

support her argument.

3 The author uses _____ such as 'dark corners' and 'open the door' to make her

points more visual and so more memorable for her readers.

4 Towards the end of the comment, the author makes her call-to-action more effective by using

_____ with the repetition of 'p' when she says "asking social media companies to

put public safety before profits".

5 The author begins and ends her comment by talking about the benefits and dangers of modern

technology, this use of _____ emphasizes that she is not against modern technology

itself but thinks it needs to be safer for children.

2 Now that you have completed your preparation, use your work in exercises 1a)–f) and in your student's book (pp.138–143) to complete this analysis task on the article on p. 67.

"Examine how the author presents the issue of online privacy and analyse the means used to convince the reader of her position."

Topic 1, Going deeper

Jennie: Hey, listeners. Welcome to April's O.M.P. – Oh my Pod!!! The podcast made by teenagers for teenagers. Chris O'Reilly, welcome to the podcast. So you came here today to say something?

Chris: Hi Jennie and thanks. Yes, I wanted to say that everyone should let kids be kids.

Jennie: What do you mean?

Chris: Well, to me it seems half the world thinks we are addicted to social media, don't read books, and only think about ourselves and take selfies, all these negative things. And the other half expect us to go on demonstrations, live perfect lives, and, like, save the world.

Jennie: OK. And that annoys you?

Chris: Yes. It just puts this pressure on us.

Jennie: What kind of pressure?

Chris: Well, on the one hand we feel we have to prove the negative things aren't true, you know? That we *do* still read books, we're not *always* online, and we're not just posting selfies and stuff.

Jennie: I see what you're saying, but isn't that just the way it is? Some older people *never* understand teenagers. That's not really new, is it?

Chris: Maybe not. But on the other hand, there's this pressure on us to be some kind of ... kind of ... like ... superheroes! Look at Greta Thunberg with her school strikes, and, you know those teenagers in America ... em ...

Jennie: Do you mean *March for our Lives?*

Chris: Yeah, those kids marching against gun violence in schools. I mean, don't get me wrong, I think they're great, I do, but it feels like we all have to wear second-hand clothes, become vegetarian, and go out on the streets. And if you don't, then you're some kind of bad person.

Jennie: Hang on, Chris, I don't think you're right there.

Chris: Well maybe they don't _say_ that, like, to your face. But they do make you *feel* that way. Someone unfriended me on Facebook because I said I was tired of the school strikes. I mean, don't we have enough to worry about? Getting good grades and fighting with parents ... you know ... just being a teenager.

Jennie: Yeah, but something like climate change will affect us teenagers much more than, say, grownups. Don't we have the right to protect our future? We can't ignore it just because we have homework to do.

Chris: It's too much, Jennie. I read that in America a lot of teenagers are suffering health problems because of stress or low moods. Twice as many as ten years ago!

Jennie: That's not good. But ...

Chris: I think we expect too much from ourselves. My main point is that we're still just kids. We can recycle and do positive things in our daily lives, yes. But we don't have any real power yet and expecting us to change the world – it's expecting us to do the impossible.

Jennie: But like you said, we can do the small things – get our parents to drive less and cycle more. We can eat less meat. We don't all have to be another Greta Thunberg. But we can change how each of us treats the environment.

Chris: Look, Jennie, you're doing it now, too, talking about the planet. When I take my exams, I hope to go to college so I can get a good job. Youth unemployment has been growing since 2005, Jennie. There are more and more young people now – like my older brother – with *no* jobs. Let me focus on applying to college, not saving the world.

Jennie: You don't think that's a little selfish?

Chris: Well, yeah, a bit. But I don't mean I'm more important than all those other issues, I'm just talking about the timing. When I'm an adult with a job and money, _then_ I'll do my part.

Jennie: OK, Chris. I think we'll have to agree to disagree on some issues. But I think you're right about the stress issue. It's important for you guys to know that if you're feeling stressed out and worried about things, then talk to someone – your friends, your parents or your teacher.

Chris: Yeah, Jennie, that's good advice.

Jennie: Well, Chris, thanks for coming in today and sharing your point of view. OK, guys, let us know what you think by posting your comments. [FADE OUT] I'll see you next week, when we'll be talking about the what's hot on social media.

Topic 2, Going deeper

Reporter: New plans to reduce city traffic and encourage Londoners to leave their cars at home have sparked bitter conflict.

Residents of the Hackney area in the north inner city of London were not given much warning when they discovered that city authorities had decided to turn their district into a low-traffic neighbourhood – or LTN. LTNs block motor traffic from side streets with physical barriers such as flower boxes or bollards. Residents can still drive to and from their homes, but they may have to take a longer route. Cameras with car number plate recognition can spot drivers who do not live in the neighbourhoods and they have to pay a fine. The theory is that by reducing the amount of road space for cars, people will find other ways to make short journeys. As almost half of car journeys in London are less than two miles, the hope is more people will walk or cycle, which means less pollution, less congestion, quieter, safer streets and healthier citizens.

On a rainy Saturday afternoon in December, however, a convoy of cars driven by Hackney residents set off from the district and made their way to the town hall, beeping their horns and moving slowly, in protest against the LTN. The protesters don't all have the same reasons for being against the project. Some protesters are angry that the local authorities did not include them in decisions which affect their daily lives: the restrictions can reduce the quality of life for elderly and disabled people. Lives can be put at risk if emergency vehicles such as ambulances cannot reach accidents as quickly. Others feel they are victims of a war against motorists. Another group of protesters think the project increases gentrification and will raise house prices. They say that wealthy neighbourhoods have been chosen as low traffic areas, forcing cars to drive through poorer districts. Professional delivery drivers and taxi drivers also took part in the protest saying LTNs will destroy their jobs.

A member of the city council defended the project. He said surveys show that a large majority of Londoners support environmental policies which reduce pollution and help meet targets to lower greenhouse gases. According to him, people start complaining when those plans make their day-to-day lives more inconvenient. He questioned why motorists should control one hundred per cent of the streets when seventy per cent of households in Hackney do not own a car. He said the streets were not chosen to benefit wealthy areas, but where the most congestion happens. He admitted that house prices may increase in LTNs and some may view this as a sign of gentrification, but the reality is LTNs are healthier places to live in. He also said that local communities could and should be included more in deciding future plans.

But do low-traffic neighbourhoods actually have the effect their supporters claim? Being relatively recent developments in London, the results of the first studies are not clear. One study showed traffic on main streets has risen, while another showed traffic overall had gone down. More time is needed before we know for sure.

Topic 3, Going deeper – part one

Ari Shapiro: We're joined now by Linda Holmes, who hosts NPR's Pop Culture Happy Hour podcast. Hi, Linda.

Linda Holmes: Hi, Ari.

Shapiro: You were live-tweeting this interview last night. Run through some of the biggest revelations for us.

Holmes: Well, there were certainly, you know, a couple of details of their lives together that were on the lighter side – the fact that they legally married, you know, more privately a couple of days before their big, splashy royal wedding. They talked about that. They talked about the fact that their baby who's due this summer is a girl. They gave, certainly, as you said, more information about how hard they had tried to get more support from the palace about the media harassment of Meghan.

But I think what landed the most vividly were really two things. One was how much they both felt the family not only wouldn't deal with the racism that Meghan was facing as a biracial woman – her father is white, and her mother is Black – but the family was part of it. They said that at least one conversation happened between Harry and someone in the family – they would not say who – in which the person sort of inquired about what their children's skin color might be and, you know, how dark they would be and how that would look. So that was one, I think, big thing. And the other big thing was Meghan talking about having had a serious mental health crisis, including pretty serious thoughts of suicide.

Topic 3, Going deeper – part two

Shapiro: The conversation has struck such a chord here in the U.S., including with people who don't typically care about the royal family. Do you think that's because of these themes of racism and mental health that so many people have had experience with can relate to? Why do you think this is?

Holmes: I do. I think the racism, you know, certainly exists outside the British tabloid press and the royal family, right? Meghan feeling like she was given no support and then attacked for supposedly failing is very resonant, I think, for a lot of Black women, as are the times that she was unfavorably compared to Kate, Prince William's wife, her sister-in-law, who as a white woman was often praised for doing some of the same things, right?

And by the same token, I think when she spoke about mental health, if you've been depressed, that resonates even though her circumstances are unique. And I think for a lot of people, this interview also really helped advance the sense of the monarchy as an institution where a lot of the power lies with kind of staff, people who aren't even family members. And that institution, like a lot of workplaces and governments and media organizations, can be profoundly racist and profoundly destructive to people's mental health.

Shapiro: So speaking of media organizations, as you say, it's not only the royal family that came under a harsh light in this conversation. It was also the British tabloid press. Tell us about that.

Holmes: Yeah. Harry and other members of the family have been critical of the tabloids before. But you know, he spoke Sunday night about what he called a sort of invisible contract between the family and the tabloid press, where essentially, the family feels at the mercy of those tabloids and can't really stand up to them. He said that the firm, which is the word they sort of use to describe the kind of formal and informal power structure, really is controlled by fear of the tabloids.

Shapiro: There are so many comparisons being made today to Princess Diana's 1995 BBC interview, which people remember for this famous line about three of us in the marriage ...

Holmes: Yeah.

Shapiro: ... Talking about Prince Charles' relationship with Camilla Parker Bowles. How would you compare the role that Diana's playing to this situation today?

Holmes: Well, Diana loomed very large over this interview, I think. For one thing, you know, Harry said he's been cut off financially by the family. So the money that he has is actually the money that his mother left him. But more significantly, he spoke about not wanting history to repeat itself, not wanting Meghan to be hurt the way his mother was hurt, which I

think is very – you know, that's very sad and very understandable.

Topic 4, Going deeper

Julie: Hey Miriam, welcome to the podcast. What've you got for us today?

Miriam: Okay, so you know how one of the big problems right now seems to be like all the misinformation flying around?

Julie: Yeah. People are calling it an *infodemic*.

Miriam: That's right. I've been thinking about one particular situation in all this. Like, what do you do when it's somebody you love? A friend or family member who's spreading the misinformation?

Julie: Right, right. That can be tough and lead to some nasty family conflict.

Miriam: Exactly. And nobody wants that. So I've done some research into ways you can correct misinformation and cause less tension with the people you're close to.

Julie: Brilliant.

Miriam: OK, well. Let's make up an example – I don't want to spread any more misinformation by accident...

Julie: No, let's not do that.

Miriam: OK. Imagine your auntie posts a story that ... em ... listening to Taylor Swift music can make you go blind, right?

Julie: [Laughs] O-K...

Miriam: And you're a big Taylor Swift fan.

Julie: Yep! So I jump in and say that's crazy. My auntie is embarrassing herself.

Miriam: No, no. Your auntie loves you, right? So, instead, you say stuff like, I understand that you're sharing this because you care about me. But there's a lot of information out there and it's hard to know what to believe.

Julie: OK, so your first reaction is: I know that you care about me, Auntie.

Miriam: Yes. No insults, no negativity. It should be a dialogue. Don't just say: That's wrong, that's crazy. Instead, you know, you could try saying: Well, that thing you sent me was interesting. But I've been reading some other stuff that says it's not exactly

right. Do you mind if I send you an article to read? And I'd love to read the report that you found, too.

Julie: Ahh... I see. So you're showing that you have an open mind and you're ready to listen?

Miriam: Yes, that's right. The common ground between you now allows you both to share information. And because you're open-minded, your auntie is more likely to be open-minded, too. So there's a better chance that she will read what you sent her.

Julie: I like that.

Miriam: And you should also ask questions. So you ask your auntie: how do they think that Taylor's music can do that? By asking questions, you can help people think more about what they believe. They might find out that the misinformation actually makes no sense when they think more deeply about it.

Julie: Mm...

Miriam: If they see that by themselves, they're more likely to think again and maybe realize that they were wrong.

Julie: And it's always easier to accept that we're wrong when we discover it ourselves, instead of being told by someone else.

Miriam: You've got it.

Julie: This is good. Anything more?

Miriam: Sure. So your auntie posted that story and you want to give your auntie, you know, *twenty* reasons why her story isn't true, and you give lots of statistics and expert research, etc etc and so on and so forth.

Julie: Right. You shoot down the misinformation with the *power of truth and science!*

Miriam: Not so fast, Julie. The original misinformation was simple and easy to remember:
Listen to Taylor Swift – Go blind. So avoid long and complicated explanations of why they're wrong. Keep it short and simple.

Julie: Mm... OK I can see how that makes sense.

Miriam: Yeah. And there's more. When you are correcting the misinformation, don't repeat it in the correction itself.

Julie: So let's stay with the Taylor Swift example.

Miriam: I want to correct it so in my social feed I post:
Listening to Taylor Swift doesn't make you go blind because blah blah blah. You see? I'm repeating the original misinformation...

Julie: And maybe people who haven't heard it before, well, they're hearing it now?

Miriam: Yes, so you're accidentally spreading it but by repeating it to the friend or family member who started it – you're actually reinforcing it – making it stronger in their brain, too.

Julie: Right. So when we're correcting the misinformation ...

Miriam: Be careful not to repeat the false part.

Julie: OK.

Miriam: One more thing. Right, let's say your cousin Mike already corrected your auntie on social media...

Julie: Yeah, OK, my cousin got there first so I don't need to make auntie feel worse by adding my comments?

Miriam: The opposite actually. By adding your comments to your cousin's then it's not just a one versus one – you're supporting both your cousin *and* your auntie. We need to move away from looking at correcting people as a negative thing to get into a big fight over, but more as a positive thing.

Julie: Right. So correcting misinformation is a way that we can protect each other...

Miriam: ...together.

Julie: Well, Miriam, I have to say I found that very helpful. Thank you.

Miriam: You're welcome.

Julie: Of course. And to any Taylor Swift fans – or Swifties – out there. We love Taylor, we do.

Track 06

Skills pages: Dealing with listening tasks

Host: This is Gen Z and Democracy, a student podcast. Today's topic is trust and the government. I have Jamal, from Cincinnati, and Lindsay, from Boston, here with me. So guys, do you think there's like a difference here in the US between having trust in local government versus the federal government?

Jamal: Well, where I live, we've had like four council members get arrested now. They made secret deals with developers or builders, or something. That's, like, pretty bad. And you see the same in the federal government, I think. You have politicians resigning because they weren't honest and tried to hide bad stuff. So I can't say I have much trust in either local or national government. But if there is one difference, it's that I can at least have a *little bit* more influence over local politics and, like, go to city hall meetings and stuff like that.

Lindsey: Yeah, I agree with Jamal – about corruption and I think a lot of people would say that they trust local government more. There's a greater chance you might know a local politician. Knowing the person, where they grew up or come from or whatever – that means you can have more trust in them. But on a national level, that personal element is missing.

Host: Do you think there's something that the government can do to, like, get more trust?

Jamal: Absolutely. Every identity, every interest should be represented in the government. The people making decisions should be like the people who are affected by those decisions. So if something affects people in my community – people of colour – then the people choosing should be people of colour, you know? People will have more trust if they know that the ones with power have the same goals and interests as them.

Lindsey: Yeah, I agree with that. But you know what I think? We always see the government or politicians having these press conferences on TV with journalists asking them questions and, like, they can never answer a simple question, you know? So I think, instead of journalists, it should be *real* people, like you and me, asking the questions, you know? And, like, have it live on TV and have the regular people ask the government about the stuff that's important to them.

Host: Thanks, guys. Before you came on the podcast, I asked you to imagine if you had magic powers and could change one thing in our political system with a click of your fingers, what would it be? What did you guys think of?

Lindsey: My thing is kind of related to what Jamal was saying about representation. We won't have people from every identity in government if there aren't candidates standing that we can vote for, you know? And what's stopping more Native American or LGBTQ or poor people getting involved is the fact that you need so much money to do things like run an election campaign. I mean it's so expensive! I just think that nowadays you have to be rich yourself or ask big companies for money if you want to get elected.

Host: So what's your magical solution?

Lindsey: Well I think that there should be public money available for people to stand for election to the House of Representatives and the Senate. So if you're poor but you want to represent your community you can get funds to pay for a campaign. And not only that. There should be, like, a restriction on how much money a candidate can spend on their campaign – a maximum – so some millionaire can't just come along and win because he – or she – has more money.

Host: That's interesting, Lindsey.

Lindsey: It would take some of the corruption out of it, and politicians would be more free to do what we need them to do and not just what big corporations want. You know?

Host: Thanks, Lindsey. So what did you think of, Jamal?

Jamal: Well, let's look at the Senate. Each senator serves for a six-year term. So let's say I'm a senator, elected in 2020. Maybe in 2024–25, I start worrying about being re-elected and in 2026 I'm in full campaign mode. Well, at least I got some work done in four or five years. But look at our House of Representatives! If I'm elected in 2020, I'm already worrying about re-election because I'll have another election to fight in 2022. That's crazy! Democrats and Republicans in the House are just... they're always in campaign mode, you know what I mean? Just out to make the other side look bad. Like, I wonder when politicians, especially in the House, get the time to think about solving the problems the country and the planet are facing.

Host: OK, so what's your solution?

Jamal: I think we should make the elections for the House of Representatives happen on a four-year cycle – not two years – and have them at the same time as the presidential. If we do this, the politicians can concentrate at least a little more on the long-term issues we have. Like, without an election always around the corner, you know, Republicans and Democrats can stop fighting each other so much, and they'll have more time to work together, you know? More cooperation and less competition.

Host: And the Senate?

Jamal: I'd leave that alone – I don't think we need to change those elections.

Host: Two very interesting ideas. Lindsey and Jamal, thank you. But don't go away because we just have to take a short break and we'll go on with the discussion after that [fade out]

Bildquellen

Textquellen

Verfasser	Peadar Curran
Redaktion	Daniel Shatwell
Redaktionelle Mitarbeit	Christine House
Verlagsredaktion	Shaunessy Ashdown
Umschlaggestaltung	Rosendahl, Berlin
Coverfoto	Shutterstock/Lewis Liu
Layout	Klein & Halm Grafikdesign, Berlin
Technische Umsetzung	Straive, Chennai

Andere Begleitmaterialien für Schülerinnen und Schüler zu Crossover Band 1:

E-Book des Schülerbuchs   ISBN 978-3-06-452110-0

www.cornelsen.de

1. Auflage, 2. Druck 2025

Alle Drucke dieser Auflage sind inhaltlich unverändert und können im Unterricht
nebeneinander verwendet werden.

© 2021 Cornelsen Verlag GmbH, Mecklenburgische Str. 53, 14197 Berlin,
E-Mail: service@cornelsen.de

Druck: Drukarnia Dimograf Sp. z o.o., Bielsko-Biała

ISBN 978-3-06-452112-4

PEFC-zertifiziert
Dieses Produkt
stammt aus
nachhaltig
bewirtschafteten
Wäldern und
kontrollierten Quellen
PEFC/32-31-076   www.pefc.pl